THE PUREFOY LETTERS

The
Purefoy Letters
1735-1753

Edited by
L. G. MITCHELL

ST. MARTIN'S PRESS
NEW YORK

AFFILIATED PUBLISHERS: Macmillan Limited, London
—also at Bombay, Calcutta, Madras and Melbourne

Printed in Great Britain

To
J.D.P. and R.A.P.

Acknowledgements

Practically any book on a modern historical theme is only made possible by an almost predatory calling on the help and assistance of other people. Certainly, the present author has incurred debts of many kinds which should be acknowledged. To the Master and Fellows of University College, Oxford, I owe the opportunity for completing this work. Dr T. M. Parker and A. F. Butcher Esq. of the same college gave me invaluable advice on historical periods with which I was unfamiliar. R. U. Young Esq. and C. R. Buttery Esq. lent assistance of a more practical, but nevertheless essential, kind. Above all, I have to thank Geoffrey Purefoy, the present owner of Shalstone, who enthusiastically entered into this project, and who gave all the co-operation that any writer could wish for. I would like to thank formally all these people, and I hope that they may read this book with pleasure.

Contents

Introduction

THE Purefoy family came into possession of the manor of Shalstone in Buckinghamshire in 1415, when a William Purefoy married Mariana, daughter of Alan de Ayete, whose family had in turn been resident there from 1280. For nearly seven hundred years, therefore, the responsibilities of ownership have remained firmly in only two families. The will marking the transfer of authority is preserved at Shalstone, and is worth quoting at length:

> This indenture made between Alan de Ayete on one part, John Barten senior, John Barten junior, William vicar of the church of Stowe, David rector of the church at Shaldeston, and John Smyth of Buckingham on the other part attests . . . [that] it is the will and intention of the said Alan to the said manor of Shaldeston and to all the said lands, tenements, rents and services in Shaldeston that the said John, John, William, David and John might give the said manor and also all lands, tenements and rents and services aforesaid with all appurtenances to William Purefreye to have and hold to the said William for the term of life of the said Alan paying annually to the said Alan for his life 20 marks at 4 terms of the year by equal portions. And after the death of the said Alan that the said John, John, William, David and John might give and concede to the said William Purefreye the said manor to have and hold with all appurtenances to the said William and his heirs . . . The Said Alan wills also that the said John, John, William, David and John might give and concede to the said William Purefreye and his heirs in perpetuity all other lands, tenements, rents and services which they have by gift and enfeoffment of the said Alan in the said will of Shaldeston, held by him by sufficient security that the said William might provide annually during the next 12 years a suitable chaplain to celebrate divine service for the soul of the said Alan and the souls of his mother and father and

all the ancestors, relations and benefactors of the said Alan. To which
things testified by the indentures we place our seals in turn. Dated at
Shaldeston 2nd March 1415.[1]

The estate in question lies some five miles to the north-west of Buckingham and only a mile or so from the great house at Stowe, which, under the
management of Lord Cobham, represented the major political influence in
that part of the county in the first half of the century. Shalstone itself is
surrounded by the parishes of Biddlesdon, Westbury and Water Stratford,
all of which predictably make several appearances in the Purefoy correspondence. Brackley, Towcester, Bicester, Aylesbury and Banbury were just
within reach in a day's journey, and these towns effectively delimit the area
in which the Shalstone family would trade, make visits and amuse themselves. It was an overwhelmingly rural community, serviced by a network
of small craftsmen and tradesmen in the towns. The leaders of opinion
naturally consisted of the landowning gentry, together with a sprinkling of
successful and educated lawyers, doctors and clergymen. It was a tight,
largely self-sufficient, community, whose basic social and political attitudes
changed barely at all in the eighteenth century. Elizabeth Purefoy and her
son Henry write with the confidence of people living in an assured and
immutable environment.

A contemporary description of the parish is given by Browne Willis,
the Buckinghamshire antiquarian, who lived only a few miles from Shalstone, and was a great friend of the Purefoy family.

> The Parish of Shalstone . . . contains 1274 Acres. The Number of Families
> is 22, and of Souls 118, as was returned Anno 1712. It was then assessed
> to the Land Tax £80. 15s. 9d.[2] The Church, which is dedicated to St
> Edward the Confessor, King of England, whose Festival is Oct. 13, (the
> Sunday after which is a Wake observed here,) is a mean structure . . .[3]

---

[1] I am most deeply indebted to Dr L. G. Black and Mr A. F. Butcher of University
College, Oxford, for their help in the translation and transcription of manuscripts.
[2] The Land Tax was one of the principal sources of government revenue throughout
the eighteenth century. Owing to the high cost of the wars against Louis XIV, it was
rarely levied at less than 3s. in the pound. In the middle years of the century, a rate of
1s. in the pound would be more usual.
[3] Browne Willis, *The History and Antiquities of the Town, Hundred and Deanry of Buckingham* (London: 1755).

At the time that the letters were written, the land was still unenclosed, and remained so until Henry's successor, George Jervoise Purefoy, secured a private Act of Parliament to that end in 1767. With an income of between £450 and £550 a year, the Purefoys could count themselves among the more substantial families of the county, and it is not surprising that Henry should have been called upon to take an active part in the public life of Buckinghamshire.

A Buckinghamshire squire of the middle years of the eighteenth century therefore functioned on three distinct levels. Most of his day would be spent in the management of the estate, which he farmed as a dynastic unit for which he was the trustee. As the major support of his standing within the parish and the county, the land had to be carefully husbanded if it was to produce a satisfactory level of income. This was particularly true of this period, as agriculture in general was struggling against low food prices and a shortage of good tenants. Secondly, because the squire was not only the landlord of the village but also the leading citizen of the parish, Henry Purefoy again and again found himself involved with the private lives, personal quarrels and criminal activities of the Shalstone inhabitants. Finally the county would expect him to sit on the Grand Jury, act at the Quarter Sessions, and divert himself in their company at the local hunt or watering place. Although London was only sixty miles away, the capital was an object of suspicion, always expensive and almost certainly peopled by profligates and swindlers. The Purefoy connection with London was limited and impersonal. For the most part, they acted in a parish or county environment, and it is hoped that the several chapters will effectively illustrate their diversity of function within these broad contexts.

THE LETTERS AND DIARIES

The 1,260 letters in the Purefoy collection cover the years 1735 to 1753, and are contained in three letter-books. They were therefore written during the administrations of Robert Walpole and the Pelham brothers, a period which Burke later characterized as involving 'a salutary neglect' of government. Faced with the substantial problem of settling in the new Hanoverian dynasty, these statesmen were anxious to do as little as possible by way of legislation, for fear of offending those entrenched interests in county and borough, on whose support the security of George I and George II depended. The Purefoy letters faithfully reflect this mood. There are only

two references to national politics in the whole collection, both relating
to the invasion of the Young Pretender in 1745. Overwhelmingly, the
letters deal with local or county matters. Even England's involvement in
war against France and Spain between 1739 and 1748 finds no echo in the
writings of a Buckinghamshire squire living only sixty miles from
Westminster.

The diaries, stretching, with a nine-year gap, from 1725 to 1756, exemplify
this tendency even more clearly. Entries for each day were made under one
of three printed headings; 'Places where I was', 'Persons I spoke to' and
'Faults'. Unfortunately, this system allows the minimum of information
to the historian. We know where Henry Purefoy went each day, but only
rarely for what purpose. We know to whom he spoke, but never the nature
of the conversation, while the minor peccadillos listed under the last heading
have no special reference to the eighteenth century, being common to human
experience at any time. Certain fixed points in Henry Purefoy's life are,
however, clear. He usually attended divine service twice on Sunday, and
took Communion at Easter, Whitsun and Christmas. Variation came in the
form of weekly visits to the neighbouring markets, the spa at Astrop Wells,
and other gentry families in the area.

More interestingly, by simply cataloguing the people Henry Purefoy
spoke to day by day, it is possible to build up a reasonable picture of Shalstone society at large. The substantial tenants on the estate, who are recorded
as having servants of their own, were dignified with the title of 'Goodman',
and were expected to shoulder the burden of the major parish offices such as
Parish Clerk, Overseers of the Poor, and Receivers of the Land Tax. Below
them were the village artisans, whose function was noted in brackets after
their names, as though more adequately to fix their station in the small,
organic society, over which he presided. Thus he regularly converses with
'Mr Steell (the Hogpoker)', 'Mr Thomas Peers (the Ratcatcher)', and
'Mr Simon Hobcraft (the Blacksmith)'. Also appearing in brackets are
any oddities of nationality or religion, which might make a man stand
outside this closed community, and therefore make him potentially danger-
ous. In 1746, for example, he encounters 'Goodman William Hawkwood
(the Quaker)' and 'Mr Wm Mack Whurr (the Scotsman)'. There was a clear
preference for what was known and familiar.

The Account Books of Elizabeth Purefoy and her son, which also span
the whole period under discussion, reinforce this theme. Village economics
figure prominently. The entry for 5 April 1743 reads as follows:

paid Goodman Daniell Burman & Aaron Gibbs Churchwardens to a
Levy at 1½ in the pound   5/4½
paid young William Strange (Overseer of the Poor) To a Levy at 2ᵈ in
the pound   7/2
paid young William Strange Constable To a Levy at an halfpenny in
the pound for carryeing the King's Baggage from Buckingham to
Northton   1/9½

The squire would also be expected to contribute generously to church
collections, and would be under an obligation of meeting the incidental
expenses to traditional village ceremonies. The processioning round the
parish boundaries in May 1740 for example cost Henry Purefoy 10/6 in
beer, hops and bread for those taking part. His meticulous detailing of local
life even extends to a complete record of his financial transactions with his
mother. A sixpence passing from one to the other was faithfully noted down.
Long hours must have been spent in the compilation of these records, and
this fact emphasizes just how self-sufficient such an eighteenth century
community was.

From the combined evidence of letter-books, diaries and accounts, it is
possible to build up a comprehensive picture of a gentry family set in the
context in which it would have considered itself important. Power and
authority for them stretched out in concentric circles from the parish to
the county and then to the capital, but the larger the circles became, the less
telling was the influence of the squire, and the more uneasy or alarmed he felt.
Smollett's Squire Bramble, Fielding's Squire Western, and Addison's
Roger de Coverley would all have subscribed to this view. Henry Purefoy
visited London irregularly, and, as the diaries and letters suggest, his reaction
was a mixture of wonder at the new Westminster Bridge and an ingrained
suspicion that the sharp practices of the Londoners would involve him in
financial loss at some stage. He and his mother approved of London fashion,
but feared London prices. The chapters on their dealings with London effectively demonstrate this ambivalent attitude. In marked contrast, the parish was
the social context in which they were all-powerful and totally competent.

ELIZABETH AND HENRY PUREFOY

Elizabeth Purefoy was widowed in 1704, when she was thirty-two years old,
and then lived on for a further sixty-one years. She came from a Hertford-

shire family named Fish, and some of her kinsmen appear in the correspondence as co-heirs in her family's property.[1] As her letters to tradesmen and neighbours indicate, she was a woman of determined character, with a very clear view of what her rights might be in any given situation. Her relations with the rest of her family are particularly revealing in this respect. She was always very ready to threaten inefficiency or suspected dishonesty with the law, and was as careful as her son in her personal accounting. She clearly dominated her son completely, and the only suggestion in the letters that Henry might marry was met with a polite refusal. Further, in order to ensure that posterity had a correct view of her personality, she had a marble monument erected in Shalstone Church while she was still alive, and may herself have written the inscription that appears upon it. She also planned her own funeral, which cost no less than £110 1s. 9d. or approximately a quarter of a year's income. The personality of this forceful lady is best captured in the inscription on the monument:

> She was an Woman of Excellent Sense and Spiritt
>   Prudent and Frugall
> As well as a true ffriend To the family She married into.
> And was moreover endued
>   With all Those Graces and Virtues
>   Which distinguish and Adorn
> The good Wife The good Mother and the good Christian.

Henry Purefoy was born in 1697, and predeceased his mother by three years, dying in 1762 at the age of sixty-five. The earliest information about him concerns his stay at Oriel College, Oxford, from 1720 to 1723. There is no evidence that he took a degree, but that would not have been unusual in this period. A university career was intended to provide that smattering of polite learning necessary for a gentleman to take his place in society, and nothing more. A sketchy account book is the only evidence of his activities; the following are typical entries:

May ye 15th 1720. Paid Mr Weeksy then the sume of four pounds & four shillings for halfe a years Tutoridge.

---

[1] The family had been in Hertfordshire since the sixteenth century, and Mrs Purefoy's father, Leonard Fish, had also become involved in London property. This explains the Purefoy interest as landlords in houses in Hatfield and London, which are discussed in the correspondence.

April ye 4th 1723. I paid Monsieur Leffebvre my ffrench master half a Guinea for a Month's teaching and in full to this time.

July ye 30th 1723. I paid to Severall persons underwritten as follows.

To Goody Erle In full	o – 6 – o
To Stubbs for Strapping Shoes	
In full	o – 3 – o
To Sedgly ye Barber for Shaving.	
In full	o –17 – 6
To Goody Robinson for 'tendance.	
In full	o – 9 – o
To Christian Newman for Washing & bedmaking	
In full	3 – o – o

These three years, however, represent the longest period that Henry Purefoy spent away from Shalstone, and must therefore be considered as an important influence, given the rather narrow range of experience on which he could draw.

Certainly he bore little resemblance to the prototype of the eighteenth century squire drawn up by Macaulay, whose only reading would be from the Bible and the fishing manuals of Izaak Walton. Purefoy was a regular subscriber to the *Gentleman's Magazine*, the principal purveyor of London politics and information, and to the *Abstract of Acts of Parliament passed this last Session*, which suggests that he took his legal responsibilities as a magistrate seriously, and tried conscientiously to keep up with changes in legal practice. Much of the Shalstone library was dispersed after the death of Mrs Purefoy, but a list of some of the volumes known to have been represented will give some idea of their wide range of interests:

A Guide to Juries, setting forth their Antiquity, Power and Duty, from the Common Law and Statutes. By a Person of Quality (London: 1699)
The Elements of Euclid (London: 1720)
The Secrets of Physick and Philosophy (London: 1633)
The Comedies of Plautus (London: 1739)
Bibliotheca Legum (London: 1742)
History of the Rebellion (London: 1745)
The Attorney's Practice Epitomized (London: 1746)
History of our National Debts and Taxes (London: 1751)

B

The local bookseller was a certain James Paine of Brackley, to whom a stream of letters were addressed throughout these years, of which the following may be taken as typical.

Shalstone,
January the 6th, 1747.

Mr Paine /

The Plautus you sent me has only three of the Comedies translated, whereas I hoped Echard had translated all his Comedies. If he has, let me have the rest of them. Hobb's Thucydides was very lately to be had at one Samuel Birt's in Ave-Mary-Lane. I return the Terence again. It is so badly bound, I don't care to let it have a place in my study, but desire you to get me one that is better bound. I have received the Quintus Curtius, wch I like very well, &, desiring you to accept of the compliments of the season, am

Your humble servant
H.P.

For /
    Mr James Paine
        at Brackley /
            This.

From such letters, it is quite clear that Henry Purefoy would count himself among the most enlightened members of Buckinghamshire society, and as someone eminently equipped to play a full part in the running of that community.

In more general terms, the character of the Purefoys emerges clearly from a reading of the letters. Very much in accord with the prevailing mood, the Purefoys saw social life as an intermingling of rights and duties. Society held together if everyone did their duty towards social inferiors and superiors within a little-changing, hierarchical framework. Recalcitrance of any kind would be threatened with the law. They would patronize the same London tradesman over a period of years, but never allowed familiarity to be an excuse for faulty service. Equally, while they were anxious to ensure that their tenants enjoyed the full measure of their rights, defaulting on rent payments brought immediate threats of distraint. In the difficult economic circumstances of the early eighteenth century, only caution and a jealous guardianship of traditional rights would ensure that position and status would not be lost.[1] The Purefoys were intelligent members of a ruling, landowning class, which understood very well that its prominence rested on the prompt performance of duty and the immediate defence of rights. The following chapters illustrate how and in what context these two considerations were worked out.

---

[1] For a fuller discussion of the economic and social background to the Purefoy letters, see A. Johnson, *The Disappearance of the Small Landowner* (London: 1909); T. Ashton, *An Economic History of England in the Eighteenth Century* (London : 1955); and G. Mingay, *English Landed Society in the Eighteenth Century* (London: 1963).

1

The Parish

THE parish was for the eighteenth century squire a private empire, in which he enjoyed the privileges and responsibilities of status, as the major land-owner and first citizen in the community. The letters in this section are so grouped that they illustrate the several agencies through which the authority of a squire could be felt and made effective.

Letters 1–6 deal with the responsibilities of being the parish's leading citizen. In any dispute with neighbouring communities, in any legal action which the parish might feel compelled to undertake as a body, or in any negotiation with London or the outside world at large, the squire would naturally be expected to give a clear lead. In many cases, this might involve him in a considerable personal expenditure of money, but it was an unavoidable corollary of holding the respect of the parish. The eighteenth century had a very clear idea of what was involved in 'supporting the dignity' of an office or position, and was censorious about those who failed in this responsibility. If the Purefoys were to command attention in the parish and among their peers in the county at large, the kind of burdens described in the letters had to be shouldered.

The parish priest was second only to the squire in local standing, and letters 7–18 deal with the Purefoys' relationship to the incumbents of Shalstone. A close understanding between squire and Rector was essential. Just as the villagers were expected to take their political and legal values from the first, so they were lectured on their spiritual and moral prospects by the second. The union of the two made for an almost insurmountable system of control. If, however, the two should find themselves at logger-heads, life would be far from easy. The death of the Shalstone incumbent in 1742 and the appointment of a successor was, therefore, a matter of the highest importance for the Purefoy family. They had to be quite sure that the man they finally settled on would not, once safely installed, strike out on independent lines of action.

The diaries confirm the view that the Purefoys took their religious observances seriously. They went to two services every Sunday, and took Communion at Easter, Whitsun and Christmas. After the amenable Mr Haws became Rector in 1742, divine service was usually followed by dinner at the manor house or Rectory, to which the Parish Clerk and his wife would sometimes be invited also. This dinner provided the necessary forum for discussing village affairs, and the diners constituted a sort of village establishment by virtue of their wealth, birth and literacy.

Letters 19–25 deal with the Purefoys' relationship with the respectable inhabitants of the parish. The term 'respectable' is used advisedly, as enshrining the eighteenth century belief that people so designated would never apply to the village authorities for poor relief, would never, in other words, involve the community in expense. They are dignified with the title 'Goodman' or 'Goodwife', are known to have employed servants of their own, and are the principal tenants of the Purefoys or, as carpenters and wheelwrights, are the village artisans serving a rural community. The farming families of Penell, Franklin, May and Friday make frequent appearances in the diaries, as does 'Simon Hobcraft the Carpenter', 'Zachary Jordan the ploughwright', and 'Mr Hunt the Baker'. Interestingly, Shalstone was apparently more stable in the eighteenth century than in the previous two hundred years. Terriers of land surviving from 1571 and 1646 give only three names which are familiar in the Purefoy diaries, suggesting that all the other families must have entered the parish after the later date. By contrast, a terrier of 1805 lists Penells, Franklins, Mays, Fridays and Hobcrafts as still living in the parish. By this yardstick, the community over which Henry Purefoy presided was in fact becoming more and more stable.

This group of people is of the first importance, in that they provided the respectable backbone of the parish, and took on the responsibilities of the parish offices. The Parish Clerk tithed crops on the Rector's behalf, took up collections in church, was responsible for the parish records, and polished the Purefoy pew for a wage of 2s. 6d. a week. The Parish Constable had the difficult and unpopular task of making provision for the poor. Finally, the two Churchwardens, who seem to have held office on a yearly basis, were responsible for collecting both national taxes, like the Window and Land

Taxes, and also the impositions to meet local emergencies. The account books record that on 30 September 1737, Henry Purefoy 'paid Goodman Daniell Burman then for the Tax for the County Goall at 2d. in the pound'. The respectability and usefulness of these people gave them a claim to the squire's regard and protection. The scarcity of good tenants meant that the squire's authority could never be dictatorial, but rather that his relationship with this segment of village society was characterized by a mutual respect and a mutual fulfilling of obligation.

The final group of letters (26–40) deals with that submerged and impoverished element in the village, who only became prominent when their distress became a public issue. They appear in the diaries only in fleeting references to 'great Nan Woodcock the washerwoman' or 'Anne Mumford (maid to Mr Haws)'. Basically, they were treated with suspicion because at some stage they were likely to involve the rest of the parish in the expense of poor relief. By the Act of Settlement of 1662, the destitute had a right to claim assistance from the parish in which they were born, or from that in which they had last enjoyed a legal settlement. The last qualification was won by having lived quietly in a given community for a fixed term of years.[1] The Purefoys' concern over maidservants giving birth to illegitimate children stemmed primarily from the knowledge that the parish would inevitably be put to expense for an indefinite period. Equally, no stranger could be accepted into the community, and thereby be able to claim settlement in Shalstone, until his financial circumstances looked assured. The difficulties with the Jaycock and Woodcock families (letters 26–29 and 30–34) relate to the problem. They were people who had perpetually to be threatened, punished and exhorted, lest they became a permanent charge on the community. If possible, they would be forced to leave the parish altogether.

In their dealings with any element in the parish, however, Elizabeth and Henry betray a marked preference for the regular and the orderly. Any peculiarity, which might make an individual less receptive to the known methods of control, was noted in the diary. As was mentioned earlier, whenever Henry met Goodman Hawkwood, he never failed to note after his name the fact that he was a Quaker, and therefore escaped every Sunday from the influence of the squire and his priest. Equally, 'Mr Mack Whurr the Scotsman' was marked out by his curious nationality. Order and stability

---

[1] For a full discussion of the responsibilities of individual parishes towards their poor, see Dorothy Marshall, *The English Poor in the Eighteenth Century* (London: 1969).

depended on the regular functioning of traditional practice. In a countryside in which Henry Purefoy was forced to postpone journeys by creditable rumours that the road was infested by bands of armed beggars, the emphasis on order and stability was not unwise. Eccentricities of religion, nationality or situation were by implication suspicious. As the following chapter suggests, the Purefoys performed their parish responsibilities with conscientiousness and rigour, and, not unreasonably in a contractual society, expected the rest of the community to do the same.

(a) THE SQUIRE

1. H.P. to John Jones

Shalstone,
Wednesday, March the 2^d 1736.

Goodm^n Jones,

Shalstone folks have always hitherto kept in repair Evershaw lane gate next Shalstone Cowpasture, & also kept in repair the two pieces of hedge w$^{ch.}$ are on each side the gate across the end of the lane. Mr Sayer,[1] notwithstanding our keeping this gate & hedge in repair, has cut down a large ash tree out of the hedge on the right side of the gate post. Pray let me know if ever you knew Shalstone folks cut the hedge or lop any of the trees in that hedge, & if you know the reason why we kept the hedge & gate in repair, wch will oblige

Your friend & serv^t
H.P.

For /
Goodman John Jones at Wappenham /
This.

2. H.P. to Henry Sayer

Shalstone,
March the 11th, 1736.

Sir! /

Your workmen, who are ditching Evershaw lane, have cut down an ash

---

[1] The Sayer family bought the buildings and lands of the former Cistercian Abbey of Biddlesdon from the Villiers family in 1681. Over the next forty years, they proceeded to demolish buildings at such a rate that, as Browne Willis noted with obvious distaste, 'not the least Remains appear, or even the site of any Building whatsoever.' See also letter 35.

tree & the hedge at the end of Evershaw lane, adjoining to Shalstone Cow-pasture. – Shalstone folks have always kept in repair the gate & hedge there [from] time immemorial, so I look upon the tree as belonging to Shalstone.[1]– Your answer at your leisure what your intention is in this affair will oblige

Your very humble serv[t]
H.P.

For /

    Henry Sayer Esq at Billesdon /
        This d.

3. H.P. to the Rev. William Price[2]

Shalstone,
March the 26th, 1738.

Sir! /

Yesterday at Buckingham, M[r] Lucas told my servant that no asses must go on our Common for that M[r] Price[3] himself has none there, and that on Wednesday next he designs to have this cried[4] at Brackley, and on Thursday to drive the Common and take a great penalty on those asses he catches. So I believe it will be advisable for you to fetch yours away before that time in case yours are there still, for my man has been busy & han't seen them there this month. – I shall be glad to see you here any day but tomorrow, then we have appointed to go out. My mother joins with me in service & respect to you all & I am

Your very humble serv[t]
H.P.

For /

    The Rev[d] M[r] Price at
        Whitfield /
        This.

---

[1] Given the heavy demands made on timber supply from the ship and domestic building industries, the value of the tree in dispute would certainly justify Shalstone's attempts to stop its appropriation by another community.

[2] After a term at All Souls' College, Oxford, William Price became curate of Biddlesdon and vicar of Whitfield in 1692, and held these positions until his death in 1749.

[3] The Price family came to Westbury in the late seventeenth century, and the member of the family mentioned here is Campbell Price. It is worth noting that, compared to any of their immediate neighbours, the Purefoys had a residence advantage of nearly three hundred years.

[4] Hiring a town crier was the most effective way of advertising a point or article within a given locality.

4. H.P. to Mr Palmer

Shalstone,
March the 14th, 1749.

Mr Palmer /

In a cause we have between this parish & that of La^{un}ton in Oxfordshire, we ordered our attorney to attend on Councillor Wright of Oxford with a case for his opinion thereon, but, on perusing the opinion, we shrewdly suspect 'tis not the Councill's handwriting but a trick of the attorney's, so desire you will call on Councillor Wright & ask him if he ever gave or signed such an opinion as the inclosed is a copy of, for we have some of his writing here & this is not at all like it. If you can do this for me, let me know as much by the bearer & I will call on you at Brackley on your return if you will let me know by the bearer what day and hour, & will gratify you for your trouble. But if you come this way with your lobsters I shall want some, & am

Your friend to serve you
H.P.

For /
   Mr Palmer a carrier at Brackley.

5. H.P. to John Wright

Shalstone,
Wednesday, March 21st 1749.

Sir! /

The Churchwarden of this parish waits on you to know if the case he brings was perused and signed by you on the 10th day of February last. I have your hand to a case that is not at all like it, & your handwriting being produced to the parish they refuse to pay to the levy, by reason they think you never was attended with any case at all in this affair. To remove all scruples, I entreat the favour of you to satisfy the Churchwarden if ever you perused & handed such a case, which will oblige, Sir!

Your very humble servant
H.P.

For /
   John Wright Esq
     at Oxford
      This.

6. E.P. to Thomas Robotham

Shalstone,
January the 9th, 1745.

... I am sorry to hear there is such a bad distemper amongst your cows. I thank God we have not one cow amiss at Shalstone, nor within twenty miles of us only at Shenley & Newnton Longueville.[1] About 10 miles from hence, one Mr George bought a distempered cow of a London dealer &, unfortunately putting he amongst his other cows, he lost seventeen wch. were all he had. There was the same case at Newnton Longueville, but I don't hear it has spread. Our butcher Mr Ben: King told me he had 40 fat cows, the worst of them worth twelve pounds, & if the distemper should fall upon his cattle it would undo him. Before X'mas, I had of him a rump & surloin & another bit that weighted 6 score pounds the finest beef I ever eat. Our parishioners have sent a certificate to London that our cattle of all sorts are in good health, so our butter and everything we send to Town[2] from hence is highly accepted. My son joins with me in our services to yourself & Nelly, & I am

Your humble servant
E.P.

For /

Mr Robotham at the King's Head at Islington
near London.

7. E.P. to Thomas Robotham

Shalstone,
Octobr. 23d., 1742.

I desire Mr Robotham's acceptance of an hare, wch. I send you this day with the butter by Mr Meads the carrier. My son was within an ace of

---

1 Both villages are within five miles of Bletchley.
2 Even at this relatively early date, North Buckinghamshire was just one of the areas whose local economy was being complicated by the opportunity arising from the demands of London's growing population. Defoe, in his *Tour through the Whole Island of Great Britain*, repeatedly harps on this point as one of the major economic developments of the early eighteenth century.

catching another, had not poor Gip on flinging herself at the hare tumbled arse over head & hurt herself. With both our services, am in haste

Your h⸢l⸣e serv^{t.}

E.P.

P.S. Pray tell Mr Potts the newsman my name is Purefoy and not Burefoy, as he has directed.

On Tuesday last at 8 at night our rector, the Revd. Mr Townsend, departed this life.

For /

Mr Robotham . . .

London.

8. E.P. to Thomas Robotham

Shalstone,
October the 28th, 1742.

I [am] myself obliged to answer Mr Robotham's letter sooner than I intended, that you might satisfy Mr Willis that my son has pitched upon a person for the living, & that that affair is no longer in suspense – Wee shall be glad to see Mrs Robotham, & am in haste

Your humble Servant

E.P.

P.S. Our service & respect is with you both.

For / Mr Robotham . . .

London.

9. H.P. to Dr John Coxed[1]

Shalstone,
Novemb^{r.} the 7th, 1742.

Sir! /

I am favoured with yours of the 28th of last month by the hands of my

---

[1] A New College man who had arrived in Oxford only a few months before Henry Purefoy, John Coxed became Warden of Winchester in 1740, and held the position until his death in 1757.

worthy neighbour & good friend the Rev^d. Mr Edmunds[1] of Tingewick, & thank you for the friendship you still are so good as to retain for me.

I do assure you without flattery I would as soon hearken to your recommendation as to that of any gentleman alive were there real grounds for it, but Mr Dalby[2] has behaved so boisterously in his neighbourhood that I am sorry to tell you I dare not present him to my living at Shalstone. If you should ever chance to visit your native County of Oxon, or at least that part of it where Mr Dalby has resided, if you please to enquire his conduct, you will find I am abundantly justified in my denial on this occasion. I am Sir! with real esteem

Your very humble serv^t
H.P.

For /

    The Rev^d. Dr Coxed, Warden
       of Winchester at Winchester in
       Hampshire. By way of London.

    10. H.P. to the Rev. Wright Hawes[3]

Shalstone,
Novr. 24th, 1742.

Sir! /

I have been with Mr Land & he says he can't finish the articles[4] till he

---

1 The Rev. Francis Edmunds was a close friend of the Purefoy family, and someone whom they visited frequently. He became Rector of the neighbouring parish of Tingewick in 1720, and remained there for thirty-nine years.

2 The exact nature of Richard Dalby's delinquency is not known, but he may simply have been unreliable. We know that, in 1737, he was complaining bitterly of his situation as the vicar of Helston in Cornwall. He may have been the father of Mrs Purefoy's goddaughter, Sally Dalby, to whom a number of letters are addressed.

3 The Rev. Wright Hawes was born in 1715, and took his M.A. from Wadham College, Oxford, in 1739. He married a niece of the Mr Edmunds of Tingewick mentioned in Letter 9. The Hawes and Purefoy families became very intimate, and, in 1769, the Rector's daughter Mary married Henry Purefoy's heir, the Rev. G. H. P. Jervoise Purefoy. It must have represented a happy contrast to their experiences with Mr Townsend, and parish life must have gone more smoothly with the new Rector's arrival.

4 It was not unusual in the eighteenth century for a lay patron to ask a new incumbent to subscribe to an agreed series of conditions. A willingness on the part of the incoming Rector to resign whenever the squire asked him to do so was commonly formalized in this way. Clearly, after struggling with an unsatisfactory Rector, the Purefoys would be anxious to take all available precautions.

comes from London, wch will be next Monday come sennight, & he will come over with them to Shalstone the day after he comes down or the day after that, & he desires you would defer your induction till his return. Shall be glad to see you here soon & am

Your very humble serv^t
H.P.

For /
    The Rev^d. Mr Haws
      at Siresham.
        This.

11. H.P. to John Land

Shalstone,
January the 7th, 1743.

Sir! /

  Mr Haws appoints Monday morning next about 11 o'clock to seal the articles. He has looked over the draft & approves it, & I have sent it by the bearer & desire you will get it engrossed & be here with it on Monday next, as above mentioned, & take a dinner with us & then you may settle Mrs Townsend's affairs at the same time if you think proper. Bring the draft of the articles with you again, & there must be a bond for Mr Haws to perform covenants, & another bond from Mr Haws to lay out £100 in repairing the Parsonage House. Your answer will oblige

Your humble servant
H.P.

For /
    Mr Land Attorney at Law
      at Buckingham.
        This.

(b) SQUIRE AND RECTOR

12. E.P. to Thomas Robotham

Shalstone,
March the 20th, 1742.

I rece^d Mr Robotham's tre of the 15th of February last with my son's repeating watch & the rest of the things with it, as also the barrel of oysters

& the tale of fresh salmon, for all which we return you thanks. I should have wrote before this, had not Mr Willis[1] said at Mr Rodd's at Towcester that I had promised Mrs Robotham the next presentation of my son's living at Shalstone 3 years before the late Mr Townsend[2] died, & that you & Mrs Robotham promised it him, & that he never had bought the vicarage of Little Billing had it not been within distance of & a prospect to Shalstone living. I can't but resent this & thought I never would write to you more, that amongst you, you should be an instrument to make me such a base body & a country talk when I am an innocent person. Instead of going to buy boots at Northampton, I understand since, you went to Little Billing to dispose of my son's living. If I should sell your beer & wine & take the money for it, you would not like it. Mr Willis has the character of a civilized person, so I must believe it to be all your own. My pleasure is that I have never yet forfeited my word on any account, nor hope I never shall. My son has been confined to his chamber these 14 weeks past, but we got him out in the coach this last week & I thank God his gout does not return. On Wednesday night last, I sent you a large hare sealed at the knot of the direction & carriage paid by Mr Meads the carrier, & this day, I send you another large hare . . . with your butter, which we desire you to accept on, & hope to retain my integrity whilst I am

E.P.

For /
    Mr Robotham . . .
        London.

13. H.P. to John Land

Shalstone,
May 24th, 1743.

Sir! /

Yesterday my tenants paid Mr Haws his tithe at Siresham. So now I desire you would get the articles engrossed and we will come over to

---

1 The William Willis in question took over the parish of Little Billing in 1741. Five years later, he became Rector of Overston, and he continued to hold both livings until his death.

2 Richard Townsend had been 'over credulously' appointed to the Rectory of Shalstone by Mrs Purefoy. His unsatisfactory relationship with the Purefoys was characterized by them as 'ingratitude', and, relieved by his death, they were clearly going to take some considerable trouble over the appointment of a successor.

Buckingham on Friday next at 4 or 5 in the afternoon & execute them[1] at Shem Baxter's.[2] Your answer by the bearer will oblige

Your humble servant
H.P.

For /
> M[r.] Land Attorney at
> Law at Buckingham.
> This.

14. H.P. to Peter Moulson

Shalstone,
October the 4th, 1747.

Sir! /

I am favoured with yours dated the 29th of last month & thank you for purchasing the lottery tickets. My mother says she leaves it wholly to you for the choice of the numbers, & desires you to send them by M[r] Jones the Buckingham carrier . . ., & send with them a pound of the best flower of mustard seed, & a leather covering to put a large quire of paper in such as you was describing here to me, & place the same to account. We want a church bible, in your travels if you should meet with a second hand one that is cheap & good, let me know the price of it or the price of a new one. I am to give it to our church. We should not trouble you in these little matters only you was so kind to offer your service. We are glad to hear M[rs] Vaughan is better & we both join in our respects & service to you all, & I am with real esteem Sir!

Your very humble serv[t]
H.P.

P.S. We have rec̃ed 10 dozen & 1 quarts, & 8 dozen & 2 pint bottles.

For /
> Mr Moulson in London.

---

1 Even so, it was a further two years before the new Rector was entrusted with the parish registers. The diary for 24 November 1745 has the following entry: 'Between six & seven o'clock in the evening, I delivered the two Register Books of Shalstone parish into the hands of John Boorten, Churchwarden of the said parish, and he immediately delivered them into the hands of the Rev[d] M[r] Wright Haws our Rector, in my kitchen of the manor house of Shalstone, in presence of William Baker, Daniel Burman, Aaron Gibbs.'

2 The Baxter family held the licence of the 'Lord Cobham Arms' in Buckingham.

15. H.P. to James Perkins

Shalstone,
March the 30th, 1748.

Mr Perkins /

Our church at Shalstone is so much out of repair & one of the main beams broke, wch is now forced to be propt to prevent its falling on the people, & unless there is a new beam the Revd Mr Haws can't repair his chancel. The pews of the church are likewise out of repair & must be repaired soon, & the church floor must be new paved with stone, & likewise the church windows must be new glazed; there must also be a new church bible. I consider the tenants have great losses in their cattle & 'tis hard times with them, so entreat you will let Mr Taylor know that if he will condescend to give an oak tree to repair the church pews & three guineas towards glazing the church windows, I will give an oak tree for a beam for the church & a church bible. Then there will be the paving of the church left for the parish to do, which will come to about four pounds besides the workmanship. I pray you'll acquaint Mr Taylor hereof as soon as possible, that you may have his answer in due time for the church must be done, & because of the time of the year for cutting the oak trees. This will oblige

Your humble servant
H.P.

For /
    Mr James Perkins at Tingewick.
        This.

P.S. The river at Huntmill between Mr Taylor & Mr Hays & me wants cleaning very much, so I am ready to join in doing it this April or at Mich̄as next as you think most proper, & I desire you will let me know your sentiments of it.

16. H.P. to James Perkins

Shalstone,
May the 8th, 1748.

Mr Perkins /

I send you underneath an estimate of what quantities of timber will be required to do the seats of the church as it was computed by a carpenter in the presence of the vestry.[1] When you come this way shall be glad to see you, & let me know by the bearer when you will order your oak or oaks to be cut down, & I will order mine to be cut for the beam & am in haste

Your humble servant

H.P.

An account of what timber will be wanting to mend the pews in the church

20 standards 3 foot high 18 inches broad 2 inches thick, wch will require 20 foot of large timber.

8 seats 1 foot broad 1 inch & an half thick, 6 foot long, & 8 back boards 18 inches broad by 1 inch & an half thick, 6 foot long, requires 24 foot of timber. Boards to mend the floors of the pews 16 foot by 10 foot, & 14 foot by 5 foot & an half – 230 foot, requires 25 foot of timber. Five sills two 10 foot, two 14 & one 16 foot long, 4 by 5 requires 12 foot of timber.

'Twill take up in all fourscore foot of timber to do the pews.

Memorandum – this was agreed at a Vestry called May the 5th 1748.

17. H.P. to the Rev. Wright Hawes

Shalstone,
March the 31st, 1744.

Sir! /

I am heartily concerned to hear of your indisposition & beg you would not venture out too soon wch may increase and lengthen your illness.

It will be no matter, if we have no church at all for one Sunday, so pray don't be uneasy on that account. I have sent you the last Evening Post. My mother & self design ourselves the pleasure of waiting on you some day next week in the afternoon, when we hope we shall find you better, & I am, Sir!

Your very humble servant.

H.P.

For /

The Revd Mr Wright Haws
at Siresham.
This.

---

[1] The Vestry, as the governing body of the religious life of the parish, was likely to consist of the Rector and all his adult male parishioners. It elected the Churchwardens, the Constable and the Overseer of the Poor, and therefore any squire would be at pains to have its co-operation.

C

18. H.P. to John Greaves

Shalstone,
Septemb^r the 19th new style[1] 1752.

Mr Greaves /

I have awaited on Mr Haws our minister ab^t your affair & he appoints Monday the 2^d day of October next new style for you or Mr Gregory to come over here, when he says you may have from him a certificate out of Shalstone Register Book of the pedigree of such of your family as are therein mentioned. Wishing you success

am
Your humble serv^t
H.P.

For /

Mr John Greaves[2] at Broughton
near Newport Pagnell
Bucks

By London

(c) THE SQUIRE AND THE VILLAGE RESPECTABLE

19. H.P. to Mr Bell

Shalstone,
April the 28th, 1736.

Sir ! /

Mary Hobcraft[3] the bearer hereof waits on you to prove her late husband's will. I presume there is no occasion for an inventory by reason there is no cattle or crop, & what effects there are they be left to her only. I entreat

---

1 By an Act of Parliament in 1752, England moved over from the Julian to the Gregorian Calendar. Since this involved the loss of eleven days, it was important for letter writers to make it clear on which dating system they were operating.

2 The Greaves family was established in Shalstone at least as early as 1646, and representatives of the family were still in the parish during Henry Purefoy's lifetime.

3 She was the widow of Simon Hobcraft, the village carpenter, and her son took over both his father's name and his father's function within the village.

the favour of you to dispatch her (if you can), so that she may be at home before 'tis dark, for she is ancient. This will oblige

Your very humble serv^t

H.P.

For / Mr Bell at
    Buckingham
      This.

20. H.P. to Mr Bell

Shalstone, May the 19th, 1736.

Sir! /

I have sent the Widdo Penell[1] the bearer hereof to Aylesbury, according to Cooper the Apparitor's summons. I ordered her to wait on you at the Visitation at Buckingham soon after her husband's death, which she tells me she did & proffered to make affidavit she was not worth £5 &c. And that you was pleased to decline administering the oath to her, but, when you had examined her, bad her give the Apparitor a shilling & told her her business was done. 'Tis very hard upon this poor woman who has 5 small children, & all her effects to the very bed she lies on were seized by my mother for rent, and the inventory came to but £3 odd shillings more than her rent, & when we came to sell some of the cattle we found, if they had all been then sold, they would not have fetched money sufficient to discharge the rent. Upon her friends' importunity, my mother permits her to go on with the stock to see if she can breed up her family in case times should mend, for otherwise 'tis impossible she should go on. The poor woman is a very painstaking person, & 'twill be very hard if she is to pay anything for process wch the Apparitor threatens her with, when she actually proffered to take the oath before you, which I chid her for not doing when she came home. I am inclined to think the old Apparitor dying (who had her shilling) occasioned this mistake from the son, who might give you a wrong information.

I am, Sir! /

Your very humble Servt

H.P.

For /
    Mr Bell
P.S. I hope you will be pleased to discharge her that she may be at home
    again at night.

---

1 The Penell family held the office of gamekeeper at Shalstone throughout this period.

21. H.P. to Mr Welchman

Shalstone,
Decemb^r the 8th, 1739.

Sir! /

Nurse Hobcraft[1] was this day buried & her money in your hands is given to her grandson by her will – desire you not to pay the money if any body should bring you the note.

I have sent the draft & desire you'll get it engrossed against next Wednesday, when I will order somebody to call for it. I am Sir!

Your humble serv^t
H.P.

For / Mr Welchman senior
Attorney at Law at Brackley
This.

22. H.P. to Alexander Croke[2]

Shalstone,
June the 5th, 1740.

Sir! /

You have this trouble on account of old Goodman Hunt [for] whom as I am informed our Overseers of the Poor have got a warrant from you to attend you at the Crosskeys as this day.

His case is this. He has taken an house & close of me at four pounds a year rent & I am to pay all parish dues. I suppose I have an unquestionable right to set[3] my estate or any part thereof as I please, & am not to be dictated to by parish officers on that occasion. I further thought it proper to acquaint

---

1 She had in fact been Henry Purefoy's nurse.
2 The Croke family of Marsh Gibbon, a parish due south of Shalstone, were neighbouring Justices of the Peace, with whom Henry Purefoy frequently co-operated and occasionally fought.
3 To lease on certain conditions.

you I am not in the least consenting to what our parish officers do on this occasion, & am with real esteem Sir!

Your very hle serv^t

H.P.

For /

    Alexander Croke Esq
       at the Crosskeys Inn
       at Buckingham
          This

23. E.P. to Mrs Shuckborough[1]

Shalstone,
Novemb^r., 1752.

Madam /

Poor old Ned May, who served me as a coachman fourteen years & was with you & your late spouse sometime in the same service, not being able to write himself, has desired me to let you know that he has been with Mr Withers about such wages as are in arrear & due to him, who says it is not in his power to pay him; and, as Ned May informs me you was so good as to make him a promise to see him paid, I hope you will stand his friend in the affair, for he has bred up a numerous family of himself (his wife dying young), & by that means is very much reduced in his circumstances as well as very far advanced in years & disabled to get his livlihood by his labour. I beg the favour of an answer to this that I may not trouble you with another letter, and am Madam

Your very humble serv^t

E.P.

P.S. My son desires to join with me in our compliments to yourself & Dr Shuckborough

For /

    Mrs Shuckborough
       at Dr Shuckborough's at
          Warwick
             in Warwickshire
By London.

---

1 This was Anne, widow of Campbell Price of Westbury, Bucks (see Letter 3). In 1749, she married Dr Charles Shuckborough, who ten years later succeeded his cousin as the 5th baronet of Shuckborough Park, Warwickshire.

24. H.P. to Christopher Rigby

Shalstone,
March the 6th, 1753.

Sir! /

My mother's cookmaid, Sarah Bessant the bearer hereof, was set on by three men who bid her stand & deliver her money as she came from Banbury Fair. Nicholls, as she says, held the horse's bridle whilst Boyle rifled her pocket for money, but she had none about her so lost nothing. The man who was with her, his horse brushed by them & got of[f]. This man & she are served with subpoenas to appear at your assizes as this day, but the man & she are both afraid they will attempt to force them to prosecute these highwaymen, which will be more expence than she will be able to bear. It will be a great charity in you to put her in a way how to avoid being a prosecutrix, &, if they should choose to make her an evidence only, to instruct her how she may get her charges bore for coming hence to Northampton, both for loss of time & as a poor witness. This will much oblige, Sir!

Your very humble servant
H.P.

For /

Christopher Rigby Esq.
This.

P.S. The man who served the subpoena on Sarah Bessant said his name was John Brown. He erased the word Barrett in the Writ, & instead therof put Bessant. Q$^{rie.}$ whether this is not forgery in altering a name in the body of a writ after it is delivered out of the office.

25. H.P. to the Revd Mr Williams.

Shalstone,
March the 31st, 1753.

Revd Sir! /

The Widow Penell complains that you break up her mounds on the Sabbath & threaten to cut her gates if she locks 'em, & that you insist on having an horse way through her grounds. I can assure you there is no horse way there & must desire you to desist & not come there, for the woman is about to hayne[1] her ground.

---

[1] To mow.

I have also a complaint of my own to make to you. I am informed you have lately brought the Buckingham Hounds on hunting in Shalstone Cowpasture & my Open Coppice. This is what nobody has yet offered at before you at this time of the year, for those two places are very strong cover & protect the hares in their breeding, & I never go there myself nor permit anybody on my account to go there after February. If you go on destroying the hares at this rate & disturbing them in their cover whilst breeding or suckling their young, we shall have none left, so I desire you will not come any more into Shalstone Cowpasture or the Open Coppice this season, & as soon as I hear Mr Greenvill[1] is come down I will wait on him about it, & desire no other reason but to be

Your friend & serv^t
H.P.

For /

The Revd Mr Williams
     at Buckingham /
          This.

(d) THE SQUIRE AND THE VILLAGE DISREPUTABLE

26. H.P. to Alexander Croke

Shalstone
March the 2nd, 1737.

Sir ! /
    I entreat the favour you will get Mr Pillsworth's hand to the order for the removal of the Jaycocks as well as your own thereto,[2] which will oblige

Your very humble serv^t
H.P.

For /

Alexander Croke
     Esq. at Marsh /
          This.

---

1 The Grenvilles of Stowe, as Earls Temple and Viscounts Cobham, were the leading family in North Buckinghamshire, and would be the natural arbiters in a case of this kind. Their house at Stowe was within two miles of Shalstone, and a walk in its grounds was a common form of relaxation for the Purefoys.
2 The signatures of two J.P.s were required before any family could be forcibly removed to the parish of their birth or of their last legal residence or settlement.

27. H.P. to Edward Davis

Shalstone
March the 5th, 1737.

Mr Davis /

Two of our parish officers were at your house on Sunday last & you was unfortunately from home, so that they could not prevail on Mrs Davis to promise them to give her attendance at our Quarter Sessions at Aylesbury, to give in evidence what she knows in relation to Jaycock's settlement. She alleged you was not at home, & seemed to be uneasy at the undertaking a journey at that distance. But the parish officers told me they received so much civility that if we could contrive a way for her coming in safety that she would comply with coming without any compulsion, & that you or her son must come along with her in case she came at all. This encourages me to give her & you or your son an invitation to my house here for 2 or 3 days to rest her before she goes to Aylesbury, and the same as she comes back. As to the journey in particular, my mother will meet her at Northampton with the chariot, & if you will be so good as to hire an horse to have her thither double (for she says she can't ride single), we will pay the horse hire and let you know when the chariot shall be at Northampton, and we will take the same care to conduct her to Aylesbury, & from thence to Shalstone to my house, and from thence back again to your own house. Mr Pillsworth, the Counsel for Farthingoe people on the same affair, is our Counsel on this & will be chairman at Aylesbury in case it should be tried. It is his opinion they won't try it at all because the thing has been so lately determined, but he says we must be sure of our evidence, so I hope you will comply & let me have your answer that Mrs Davis will come if occasion be to give her evidence on this affair.

We must execute our order of removal of this Jaycock ten days before our next Easter Quarter Sessions at Aylesbury, so pray direct yours to me at Shalstone near Buckingham, to be left at Mr Palmer's the Oxford carrier's at Northampton. Mr Palmer sets out of Northampton every Tuesday morning for these parts, so I hope the next Tuesday after this comes to your hands we shall have your answer. The higler who lives at the little house next highgate may bring it to Mr Palmer's at Northampton, & I hope, if Mrs Davis should have occasion to come, she will find it rather a pleasure than a fatigue. I am

Your unknown humble serv^t
H.P.

For /
    Mr Davis at the
        Wadd near Sir John Langham's
           at Cottesbrook
               Northamptonshire
    Carriage paid 4^d.

28. H.P. to Edward Davis

                            Shalstone,
                  March the 23rd, 1737.

I received Mr Davis's Letter with great satisfaction that Mrs Davis will come if we should have occasion for her. If they appeal from our order, they must give us notice, which so soon as they do I will send a messenger on purpose to let you know when Mrs Davis shall come to Northampton & to what inn, & will take care every thing shall be according to yours & Mrs Davis's desire as to her journey in every respect, & am in hast
                    Your humble serv^t
                        H.P.

For /
    Mr Edward Davis . . . Cottesbrook /
        This.
    Carriage paid four pence.

29. H.P. to Edward Davis

                            Shalstone,
                  April the 8th, 1738.

Mr Davis /
    Our cause is to be tried next Tuesday or Friday at our Qr. Sessions at Aylesbury, so I entreat Mrs Davis may be at the George Inn at Northampton on Monday next at eleven o'clock, & my mother will come herself in the chariot to meet her there. And I dare say my mother will endeavour to

make every thing easy to her in her journey, &, if her son comes along with her, he will be very welcome to us. I am

Your humble serv^t.

H.P.

For /

    Mr Edward Davis . . . Cottesbrook /

      This.

The outcome of this particular affair is to be found in the following extract from the records of Buckingham Easter Quarter Sessions for 1738:

Whereas the Churchwardens and Overseers of the Poor of the parish of Preston on the Hill in the county of Northampton have now made their appeal to this Court this present Sessions from an Order or Warrant of Removal which the Churchwardens and Overseers of the Poor of the parish of Shalstone in this county of Bucks upon their complaint had obtained under the hands and seals of Alexander Croke and Thomas Parr Esquires two of His Majesty's Justices of the Peace (whereof one is of the quorum) for the county of Bucks aforesaid hearing date the eighth day of March last past whereby William Jaycock Senr. and William Jaycock Junr. were removed and conveyed from the said parish of Shalstone to the parish of Preston on the Hill aforesaid the same then appearing to the two said Justices upon an examination and enquiry made into the premises upon oath to be their last legal place of settlement of which said appeal the officers and inhabitants of the said parish of Shalstone having had due notice have now appeared to support and make good the said Order or Warrant of Removal and to prove the facts matters and things therein and thereby suggested and alleged now upon reading the said Order of Warrant of Removal in this Court upon examination of Ann Davis and several others witnesses upon their respective oaths in open court concerning the premises and upon hearing what could be said and alleged by counsel on either side for and against the said Order or Warrant of Removal and upon full debate of the whole matter IT IS THEREUPON ORDERED by this Court this present Sessions that the said Order or Warrant of Removal so made by the said two Justices as aforesaid and so much and such part therof as relates to the removal and settlement of the said William Jaycock Senr be ratified and confirmed and that so much and such part thereof as relates to the removal and settlement of the said William Jaycock Junr· be quashed vacated and discharged. And the same is hereby ordered accordingly.

30. H.P. to George Denton[1]

Shalstone
Octob: the 1st, 1746.

Sir! /

One Benjamin Woodcock has run away & left his wife & child to this parish. I entreat the favour of you to grant our parish officers a warrant to have him apprehended in any part of the County of Oxon, because Hee dodges about here from one parish to another. They will tell you the case more particularly. My mother's & my compliments wait on yourself & Mrs Denton & I am Sir!

Your most humble servt
H.P.

For/

George Denton Esq at
    Hillersden /
        This

31. E.P. to Mrs Mary Harris

Shalstone,
Feb'ry the 19th, 1751.

Mrs Harris /

We heartily condole & join with you in sorrow for the loss of your worthy spouse, & entrust the favour of you to enquire & let us know when Benjamin Woodcock the soldier comes from Ireland to see his friends at Bicester and when he is there, for he may be a material witness for us about his wife's settlement here. Pray direct your ĩre for me to be left at Mr Blencow's the ironmonger's at Brackley. If you had any flowers to spare,

---

1 George Chamberlayne was M.P. for Buckingham from 1727 to 1734. He was adopted by his uncle, Mr Justice Denton, and eventually took that name on inheriting the estate at Hillesden.

I should be glad of them. My son desires to join with me in our compliments to yourself & Mr John Blake & I am

Your friend & serv^t
E.P.

For /
    Mrs Mary Harris at
        her house at Bicester
           This.
    Carriage paid two pence.

32. H.P. to Peter Moulson

Shalstone,
March the 1st, 1751.

Sir! /

I send you this day by Jones the carrier an empty half hogshead, wch. I desire you to fill with the strongest white mountain wine; it is for my own drinking. And let me have a ĩre of advice by the post when it comes as also your account. My mother (I thank God) is better than she was but weak still. As to the soldier at Dublin, our law does not admit of any money in the affair, but, if your friend could let us know when he comes to England & if then he declares the truth concerning his wife having the bastard during his absence, he will be rewarded after the thing is decided.

If it would not be too much trouble, I desire you will buy for me & send three bottles of the tincture for preserving the teeth & two tooth brushes from Mr Greenough's near St. Sepulchre's Church, on Snowhill; as also to send a quarter of a pound of gold coloured mohair the same colour to the pattern sent for the servants' liveries. My mother joins with me in our compliments to you, & I am with all due esteem, Sir!

Your very humble serv^t
H.P.

P.S. The sack came safe.

For /
    Mr Moulson . . .
        London.

33. H.P. to Mr Harris

Shalstone,
April the 17th, 1751.

Mr Harris ! /

I desire the favour of you to enquire of one Mr Woodcock or of his sister, who is a married woman of your town, to what regiment in Ireland his brother Benjamin Woodcock belongs; for here is an woman who pretends to be his wife & is chargeable to our parish, since his being gone to Ireland has had another bastard child, & if we could prove that Woodcock has been in Ireland during that time we could make the man, who she swore the child to, keep it. Pray favour me with your answer directed for me to be left at Mr Blencow's an ironmonger's at Brackley. My mother's & my compliments are with yourself & Mrs Harris & I am

Your humble servant
H.P.

For /
    Mr Harris at his house
      at Bicester
        This
    Carriage paid.

34. H.P. to Benjamin Woodcock

Shalstone,
October the 27th, 1751.

Mr Woodcock,

Since your going out of England, our parish has maintained your wife & the boy she was brought to bed of soon after she was married to you. Since that, she has had another boy which she has laid to a person who is able to keep it, but for want of evidence on our parish's side we have hitherto been forced to maintain the child, for the man she has laid it to says you was over here in England and got it. We can't prove to the contrary, unless yourself or some of your regiment who mess with you can be here to be evidence that you were in Ireland when the child was got. If you can't get a furlow to come to England on your own affairs, if you'll let me know your Colonel or other officer's name who grant the furlows, will try to get you one. Our parish is like to suffer a great deal, for your wife said she would have another boy soon. I understand by your friends at Bicester that yourself & another person of Bicester who is in your regiment have a promise of a furlow next spring. The Sessions we propose to try this affair at are in the week next after Easter, so hope your furlow will be to be here about that time. What provoked me to write this to you was that, when your friends sent you an account of this matter, your answer was you never had a furlow nor once left the regiment since you first embarked from England, & that, if your wife laid in at the time they mentioned to you, it was with a bastard, & that you never more would have anything to say to her if you returned to England again.

Our parish will take it very kindly if you will come & do yourself & them justice in this affair. Pray let me have your answer directed to Mr Henry Purefoy at Shalstone near Buckingham in Bucks, by London, wch. will oblige

Your friend to serve you
H.P.

For / Mr Benjamin Woodcock of the hoñoble Colonel
Murray's Regiment at the Barracks near Dublin in Ireland.

35. H.P. to William Hughes

Shalstone near Buckingham
in Bucks,
October the 26th, 1746.

Sir! /

The poor people of Bidlesdon importune me so strongly that I can't forbear writing to you to acquaint you that one Flowers of Bidlesdon detains from the poor of that parish 12 of their 14 Cows Commons, wch Arthur, Lord Grey of Wilton ab^t the year 1590 gave to seven ancient cottages of that parish, & to the Vicar of Bidlesdon he gave a Mare & Colt and Bull Common. The Vicar & poor folks occupiers of those 7 ancient cottages enjoyed these Commons ever since, till a few years ago Mr Sayer pulled down 6 of the ancient cottages & erected 6 new ones in another place & took 12 of the poor folk's Commons from them but was kind to them in other respects in lieu of it. Now when Mr Sayer went beyond sea, the poor people, having then no benefit from Mr Sayer, had their Cows Commons again & set all of them but two to Flowers for 5s a year apiece, for wch Flowers paid them for till a year due last Michãs, wch he says he will not pay unless the law compels him to it. They are poor & not able to contest it at law, & I hope it will be in your power to relieve them, & Flowers to this day pays the Vicar for his Mare & Colt & Bull Common, & as the Vicar's Commons stand on the same foundation as to right & title with the poor's Commons, it is plain they have as good right to it as the Vicar, & as to the other Cows Commons belonging to the house not pulled down, Mr Sayer never took them from that house but they enjoyed them all along to this day without interruption. I desire you will lay this before Sir Robert Cotton in a proper light, & your favour & assistance will be a great charity, for I think it a pity the Poor should be deprived of their Right only because they are poor, & that any charity should be abused. Your good offices in this affair will be esteemed a signal favour to

Your unknown ĥle serv^t
H.P.

P.S. Pray your answer at your leisure
For / Mr William Hughes Attorney
   at Law near the Globe Tavern
      in Hatton Garden in Holborn London.

36. H.P. to William Hughes

Shalstone,
March the 29th, 1747.

Sir! /

I am favoured with yours of the 1st of last November wherein you kindly mention you would see the poor people of Biddlesdon their grievances redressed. They have attended Mr Flowers & he refuses to pay them & says he has been at London with you and that you will have the profits of the 14 Cows Commons distributed amongst the poor of Bidlesdon in general, without having any regard to the particular right of the 7 ancient cottages to which Arthur, Lord Grey of Wilton gave the said 14 Cows Commons.

The 12 Cows Commons wch Flowers holds are not (as I am informed) in his lease from Mr Sayer, &, if it be your will to have the matter rest as it is till you come down, I shall be glad to see you here to inform you of the poor people's right in this affair, unless you should determine it in the behalf of the seven ancient cottages before that time, & am Sir! /

Your humble servant
H.P.

For /

    Mr Wm Hughes at the Crown
        Office in the Inner Temple.
        London.

37. H.P. and others to Joseph Friday

Shalstone,
October the 25th, 1747.

Joseph Friday /

We are informed by Mr Shillingford of Buckingham that you are both able & willing to keep your family, altho' they have been a great charge & burthen to this parish ever since you have absconded.

Notwithstanding which if you will send for your family & pay the charges of their removal to you where you are, & keep and maintain them so as they may be no more chargeable to the parish of Shalstone, or allow them three shillings a week here till you can so remove & keep & maintain them, we will forget & forgive you all that is past & give you no trouble.

If you send your wife anything that we don't know of, her allowance from the parish is not at all abated for it. We hope you will act the honest part in this affair & give us no other reason than to be

Your friends to serve you
H.P.
W. Haws, Rector
James Greaves ⎫
Aron Gibbs   ⎬ Churchwardens
          ⎭
Wm Strange, Overseer of
the Poor.

P.S. We desire your answer by the post in a fortnight's time at farthest that all things may go well between us.

38. H.P. to Harry Wallbank

Shalstone,
December the 29th, 1748.

Sir! /

I desire you to enquire of Nan Woodcock (the bearer hereof) if she is able to pay you for the cure of her breast, if she is not we must give the parish notice of it – for my mother will not bear any charge thereof. Pray accept the complimts. of the season, & I am

Your humble servant
H.P.

For /
   Mr Wallbank at
      Buckingham
         This.
P.S. Pray your answer by the bearer.

39. H.P. to James Paine

Shalstone,
Novemb^r 30th, 1750.

Mr Paine/

I send you enclosed the title of a book which I desire you will send for me. Here is a farmer's son of this parish who is out of place, & has lived with a clergyman three years; he waits at table very well, & can do almost any sort of business. His master parted with him because he outgrew his wages & will give him a character. We are provided, otherwise would have him ourselves. If you hear of ever such a place for him, should take it as a favour if you'll let me know thereof, and am

Your humble servant
H.P.

For /
   Mr James Paine
      at Brackley /
         This.

40. H.P. to the Revd Mr Anselm Jones

Shalstone,
October the 26th, 1751.

Sir! /

Mr Parker the Brackley barber told me on Wednesday last that you wanted a servant boy – Our parish officer waits on you with one that I

D

think will do your business as it was described to me by the barber. He has hitherto been bred up amongst the farmers here & they give him a character of being handy and honest – if you are not already provided, I believe he will prove to your satisfaction. My mother joins me in our compliments to yourself & Mrs Jones and I am Sir! /

Your humble servant
H.P.

For /

    The Revd Mr Anselm Jones
      at Mixbury.
        This.

41. H.P. to John Low

Shalstone,
May the 5th, 1739.

Mr Low /

    There is one Catharine Poulton a servant lately delivered of a female bastard child at my house, and the parish officers have been with you to find the father of it.

    You was so kind to proffer your best endeavours to take him. I do believe according to what the parish officers say, it would be as well for your family as our parish if the putative father could be apprehended. So if you should be successful & get intelligence of him, if you would let me have a line or two from you directed to Mr Purefoy at Shalstone near Buckingham by way of London – our parish officers shall come to you. This will oblige

Your unknown friend
to serve you
H.P.

For /

    Mr John Low
      at Cold Harbour in
      Studham parish.
      To be left at the Wheat Sheaf
      Inn in Thame /
        This.

2

The County

RUNNING parallel to the duties and rights which bound Henry Purefoy to his parish were those that tied him to his county. The 'county' was not simply a geographical expression or a legal convention, but was a powerful collective opinion, which made comparisons, censured, applauded, and which, on certain occasions, had to be consulted. Broadly speaking, it was made up from the landowning and the literate, but even such individuals were still subject to its corporate power. The Purefoys were qualified by birth and wealth to be part of 'the county', and yet were very careful to earn its good opinion.

In a formal sense, the 'county' of Buckinghamshire met two or three times a year as a legal entity. It was thought proper that the collective wisdom of the gentlemen assembled on the Grand Jury should decide whether a case should actually go to trial or not. By issuing a writ of 'ignoramus', they could prevent many kinds of action from being heard in a higher court. The legal textbooks, which are mentioned as having once formed part of the Purefoy library, were therefore very necessary to enable country gentlemen to skate over the finer points of the law. As Letters 51 and 55 suggest, Henry Purefoy took his responsibilities seriously, and the diaries confirm that he was a regular attender at the Assizes. Something more than an amateur interest in the law was necessary if people were to perform satisfactorily in this context and at the more humble level of their own Quarter Sessions.

These meetings in Buckingham and Aylesbury also served another purpose. They allowed Henry Purefoy to meet the leading families of the county, who represented him at Westminster. On 8 July 1755, for example,

Henry recorded that at Buckingham Assizes he dined with the following: 'Judge Clive, Judge Birch, Earl Temple, Earl Verney, Hon. George Greenvill, Mr Geo Denton, Mr Wright of Gothurst, Mr Richard Lownes of Winslow, Mr Wilks, young Mr Wilks . . . others of the Grand Jury whose names I know not, the Viscount Say & Seall'. Not infrequently, the patronage of the Temples of Stowe or the Verneys of Claydon could expedite a law suit, secure a profitable position, or simply avert unpleasantness. In Letter 48, a breakdown in this patronage network is specifically blamed for involving Henry Purefoy in the onerous duties of being sheriff. It was at such meetings that country gentlemen would hope to be informed of the latest news from the capital, and that the London-based M.P. might learn something of his constituents' opinions.

The first half of this chapter deals with the year in which Henry Purefoy performed the functions of sheriff in his county. In what must have been a generally rather slow-moving and unhurried existence, this event must have ranked among the most important in his whole life. And yet it was one that he approached with great apprehension. The office was certainly prestigious and a clear testimony to the weight his family carried in the county. But there were also many drawbacks. The expense involved in purchasing sufficient clothes, carriages, and the accessories necessary for the office could be enormous (Letter 52). Equally a public figure had to set an example, and could therefore no longer go in for mild forms of tax evasion (Letter 53). To guard against such problems, those Buckinghamshire gentlemen who feared that they might be appointed sheriff subscribed five guineas a year to a fund, the yield from which could annually be spent by the incumbent. The rules for operating this fund are printed in full. Having failed to stop his nomination in London therefore, Henry Purefoy was anxious to establish the fact that, although his contributions were in arrears, he should still be eligible for the fund's benefits.

Not all contacts between the constituent elements of 'the county' were, however, formal. Henry Purefoy's diaries indicate an assiduous round of visits to the gentry and clergy of the surrounding parishes for the purpose of hunting or simply for an exchange of gossip. If such meetings were impeded by bad weather or distance, the necessary information and news was conveyed by letter post (Letter 75). In particular, the little spa at Astrop Wells near Banbury provided a rendezvous of some importance. The curative powers of its waters were such as to attract people from as far away as Lincoln, Oxford or London. It was quite usual for gentlemen to go on to

Astrop after doing their duty at the Assize. Henry Purefoy clearly took great pleasure in these occasions. On 25 August 1749, a visit to Astrop allowed him to meet 'Rev[d] Dr Grey, Dr Trimnell & his wife and Dau[r.] Miss Trimnell, the Lady Wills & her Son Counsellor Edward Wills, M[r] Cartwright of Aynhoe, ye Rev[d.] M[r] Herbert, M[r] ffranks, Dr Mac: Aulay & his wife, Counsellor Bell, M[r] and M[rs] Keck, the Rev[d.] M[r] Trott (vice principall of St Alban hall) and sundry other Persons whose Names I know not'. Three days later, he breakfasted with the Earl of Dalkeith. The gambling, dancing and water-taking at Astrop allowed the country gentleman to meet the people who shared with him the responsibility for administering his county.

The point which the letters contained in this chapter emphasize is a simple one. Although London lay a mere sixty miles away, Henry Purefoy's social world was almost entirely contained in conventions and attitudes of his own 'county' system. It was against these conventions that he wished to measure himself, and to be judged. He would be clear that he had a dignity or standing in the 'county', which had to be supported at all costs. Just as the parish network of relationships involved duties and obligations, the 'county' also called for effort and service, so that Buckinghamshire life would continue to run smoothly.

(a) THE SHRIEVALTY

42. H.P. to John Pollard[1]

Shalstone,
January the 8th, 1747.

Sir! /

I have received a 'tre from M[r] Sheppard[2] of Lidcot by the Bailiff M[r] Hall, in which he informs me that, at the Quarter Sessions at Aylesbury the 14th January next, will be a meeting of the gentlemen & subscribers to the sheriff's articles to nominate a committee, & to make some necessary additions to & alterations in the same. As I am very bad with a cold, I can't possible go to Aylesbury, so if you go yourself please to make my excuse to the Gentlemen,

---

1 The Pollard family had moved into the neighbouring parish of Finmere in the late 1730s. They frequently appear in the diaries as being on very close social terms with the owners of Shalstone.
2 The Sheppard family had held the office of Deputy Sheriff for some thirty years.

or otherwise do it by letter if you write. When you have paid the five guineas for me, be so good as to let me know, & I will either bring or send them to you. My mother & self desire you & Mrs Pollard to accept of the compliments of the season, & I am Sir!

Your very humble serv^t·
H.P.

For /
   John Pollard Esq. at
      Finmere /
        This.

43. H.P. to John Pollard

Shalstone,
January the 22nd, 1747.

Sir! /

    I have received advice from a friend in London that the three gentlemen, who were pricked down for Sheriffs for the County of Bucks, have all got of[f], and that Mr Campbell Price of Westbury or myself will certainly be the pocket Sheriff[1]. I must beg the favour of you to let me know whether or no I shall have the benefit of the articles for regulating the expences attending our Sheriff's office, by reason I have not paid the five guineas. If I am within the articles and shall have the benefit of them, I will not endeavour to prevent being pricked down Sheriff, but if you imagine I am not, I must write immediately to my friends in Town to use their endeavours to get me of[f]. Our best compliments attend Mrs Pollard & yourself, & I am Sir!

Your very ĥle servant
H.P.

For /
   John Pollard Esq at
      Finmere /
        This.

---

1 Traditionally, the office of the Exchequer would nominate three candidates in each county for the shrievalty by 'pricking' their names on a list of those eligible. If all three candidates escaped this duty, then the king himself would nominate. His nominee came to be known as a 'pocket sheriff'.

44. H.P. to Thomas Sheppard

Shalstone,
January the 23rd, 1747.

Sir! /

I received your letter by Mr Hall of Gawcott, & would have waited on you & the other gent. at Aylesbury but was ill of a cold. Mr Pollard told me he would pay you the five guineas for me, which I did not understand till yesterday but that he had paid it. I having an opportunity have sent you the five guineas by the bearer, & desire you would give a proper receipt for the same, wch. will oblige

Your humble servant
H.P.

For /
    Mr Thomas Sheppard, attorney
        at law at Lidcot /
            This.

45. H.P. to John Pollard

Shalstone,
Monday, Febry. 6th, 1748.

Sir! /

I last night reced a lre from Mr Sheppard of Lidcot, wherein he acquaints me that I am appointed Sheriff of our County of Bucks. As I am a perfect stranger to this affair & you thoroughly acquainted therewith, I beg I may wait on you some time today to have what information you can give me therein. I am to answer Mr Sheppard's letter tomorrow, wch. makes me the more earnest to confer with you soon about it. My mother joins with me in our compliments to yourself & Mrs Pollard, & I am Sir!

Your very hle servant.
H.P.

For/
    John Pollard Esq at
        Finmere /
            This.

46. H.P. to Thomas Sheppard

Shalstone,
February the 7th, 1748.

Sir! /

I reced yours dated the 4th instant, &, as you think it proper I should soon be sworn into my office of Sheriff, the persons in my Dedimus[1] I would have to be John Pollard Esq. of Finmere in the County of Oxon., the Rev^{d.} Mr. Wright Haws, Rector of Shalstone in our County of Bucks, the Rev^{d.} Mr. Francis Edmunds, Rector of Tingewick in the said County, Mr. Harry Wallbank of Buckingham in the said County, Surgeon, & as to the Bar^{t.} you may chuse him yourself, for now Sir Charles Tyrrell is dead I don't know of anyone of that rank near us. I desire you will sue out my Patent & Dedimus, & shall be glad to see you here on Monday next at 1 o'clock to take a dinner with me. All whom are my friends I expect should set up their horses at Mr Shem Baxter's an inn holder at Buckingham & in particular that you & my men should be there during the short continuance of the future Summer Assizes at Buckingham. I am Sir!

Your humble servant
H.P.

For /

Mr Thomas Sheppard attorney
at law at Mr Howard's in
Crane Court in Fleet Street
London.

47. H.P. to James Gibbs

Shalstone,
February the 8th, 1748.

Mr Gibbs /

Since I saw you last, I am appointed High Sheriff of our County of Bucks, & shall want to use the coach at our next Assizes at Aylesbury,

---

1 Dedimus: the official writ empowering the chosen individual to perform the judicial functions of sheriff.

wch. are 28th of Feb^{ry.} next; but one of our wheel mares is so broken winded she can't perform a journey, so must entreat you to get a new coach-mare for the wheel, which must be about 16 hands high & a strong one. This will oblige

Your humble servant
H.P.

For /

    Mr James Gibbs at Souldern
      This.
    Carriage paid two pence.

48. H.P. to Richard Grenville, M.P.[1]

Shalstone,
Feb^{ry} 12th, 1748.

Sir! /

I am favoured with both your ĩres, but did not trouble you with an answer to the first by reason I rece'd a ĩre from a friend in Town with the Gazette enclosed, by wch. I found I was appointed Sheriff of our County of Bucks, & that last Monday was the last day the King had power to nominate Sheriffs for this year, saving vacancies etc:, on which I wrote to Town to my Under-Sheriff to sue out my Patent & Dedimus to take my oath of office in the county. It is not disagreeable to me in any other respects than the shortness of time allowed me to enter on the discharge of the duty of my office, for I don't know that I have deserved such usage from anybody, having always bore a sincere good affection for my present gracious sovereign & those in authority under him. Besides it has been very unlucky in another circumstance. My mother was taken ill on 23^{d.} of October last with a mortification in her leg as Dr. Pitt & the surgeon thought was for some time incurable, but has weakened her to that degree she has been confined to her

---

1 Richard Grenville (1711–1779): He was M.P. for the county or county town of Buckingham continuously from 1734 to 1752. Inheriting Stowe from his uncle in 1749 and the title of Earl Temple from his mother three years later, he was one of the wealthiest and most influential men of Henry Purefoy's acquaintance and his natural protector in London. This rather querulous letter indicates Purefoy's annoyance that this protection had not been active or powerful enough to stave off this new responsibility. (R. Sedgwick, *The Commons 1715–1754*, ii 84). It seems a likely consequence of this patronage that Henry Purefoy would have inclined towards the Whigs in politics.

chamber ever since, & now I have so ill a state of health that I have not been out of doors for a considerable time. Had I not engaged in the 5 guinea subscription, it would have been impossible for me to have got my clothes & equipage & affairs with my Under-Sheriff in readiness by the next Assize on so short a warning. So there now remains no more for me than to return your thanks to you & my other friends for their kind endeavours to rescue me from this troublesome job, w^ch, tho' they were not successful, I believe were sincere, & I am, Sir! with due esteem

Your humble servant

H.P.

For /

    Richard Grenville Esq, Member
       of Parliam^t· in Pall Mall
          London.
    Frank /

49. H.P. to Harry Wallbank

Shalstone,
February 23rd, 1748.

Sir! /

    I understand the small pox is not at Aylesbury to do any harm, therefore desire you not to speak to Mr Sheppard to give himself the trouble of coming over here, for I design to go to Aylesbury myself if I can't get anybody to supply my place. I yesterday went to Aynhoe after Mr Brown Willis to personate me, but could not meet with him. I should be glad to procure him or anybody else to do me that favour. Pray let the bearer have some scions from of[f] your summer jenneting apple tree to graft with. Shall be glad to see you or Mr Pashler here. Our compliments attend you all, & I am

Your humble servant

H.P.

For /

    Mr Wallbank at
      Buckingham
        This.

50. E.P. to Mrs Mary Price

Shalstone,
March the 1st, 1748.

This is to acquaint Mrs Price my son is obliged to go to Aylesbury Assizes, & I should be glad of your company for about a week during his absence, if you are not otherwise engaged. If you have not a conveniency of coming, I will send the saddle horses for you about 11 o'clock on Saturday morning next, or on what other hour you shall appoint. Our compliments attend you all & your answer by the bearer will oblige

Your humble servant
E.P.

For /
   Mrs Mary Price at
      Whitfield.
         This.

51. H.P. to E.P.

Aylesbury,
Wednesday, March the 8th, 1748.

Honoured Madam /

After my thanks returned for your kind desire to know how I concluded my journey, I can now acquaint you that the day I left you I got to Buckingham exactly at 3 o'clock where I delivered your box to Mr Wallbank himself, who promised me to take particular care of it. I came to the George Inn here 40 minutes after 7 o'clock at night, so guess I was 7 hours at least on my journey, but sure I am I never made a more unked[1] or solitary one in my life, & the roads were bad enough, but I thank God I have got into a good warm bed chamber where I rest well. The judge came in here about five o'clock last Monday night. We had seventeen gentlemen on the Grand Jury, of whom Sr. Wm. Stanhope[2] is foreman, and 2 Barts. (to wit) Sr. Wm. Bowyer[3] & Sr. Charles Palmer[4], & the rest most of 'em gentlemen of figure.

1 Unked: dialect word meaning weird, strange or unpleasant.
2 Sir William Stanhope: younger brother of Lord Chesterfield, and M.P. for Buckinghamshire from 1721–1741 and 1747–1768.
3 Sir William Bowyer: the third baronet, who had held the estate at Denham since 1721.
4 Sir Charles Palmer: of Dorney Court, Dorney.

The judge leaves this town on Friday morning abt 8 o'clock, so desire you will let Goodm^n. Strange come here on Thursday night. I long to be at home with you & desire my compliments to Mrs Mary Price & any other friends who may chance to enquire after, Madam

Your most obliged & dutiful son
H.P.

For /

    Mrs Purefoy at Shalstone near
        Buckingham in Bucks
        post paid twopence
        To be sent away immediately.

    52. H.P. to Mr Fell

Shalstone,
June the 26th, 1748.

Mr Fell /

    When I saw you last, you told me you should be in this country by Midsummer Day at farthest, & that you would call on me here by that time, wch. being elapsed occasions my now desiring you to come as soon [as] possible to take measure on us – The coachman stays again – Our Assizes at Buckingham are the 18th instant, wch. are ten days sooner than they used to be, & we must have our clothes made up & brought here before that time, so I don't care how soon I saw you here, & am

Your humble servant
H.P.

For /

    Mr Fell Senior at
        Chipping Norton in Oxfordshire.
        By way of London.

    53. H.P. to Peter Moulson

Shalstone,
May the 22nd., 1749.

Sir! /

    I am favoured with yours of the 9th instant, & we thankfully accept of your kind invitation, & design to set out for London on Monday next, &

if you please to procure standing for 5 horses & a coach, wch. I was forced to register[1] on my being appointed sheriff, & shall be glad to change it for one that is light & fit to travel with & second hand but not very much the worse for wearing, if it lies in your way to enquire after one against we come to Town. We both join in our compliments to you, & I am with due esteem, Sir!

Your very humble servant
H.P.

For /
   Mr Moulson . . .
   London.

54. E.P. to Mrs Loveday

Shalstone,
July the 16th, 1749.

Madam! /

I, having occasion to use my coach & chariot at our next Buckingham Assizes, should take it as a favour if you could lend me your coach wheel harness for Tuesday or Wednesday se'nnight. If it suits with your conveniency to gratify my request, they shall be returned you on the Thursday after I have 'em & shall be taken particular care on, & I will send for 'em on Saturday next. If this can't be complied with, I hope you will excuse this trouble from, Madam!

Your humble servant
E.P.

For /
   Mrs Loveday
      at Brackley
      This.

55. H.P. to Thomas Sheppard

Shalstone,
July the 3^d., 1739.

Sir! /

I expected to have seen you here before this time & hope to see you before you give the Grand Jury notice to attend etc:, because the Grand

---

1 Registration for taxation purposes.

Jury must be served with notice in due time, & I expect to have the naming the foreman and the rest of them. Also I would speak to you about other matters. Pray don't fail to let me see you, wch. will oblige, Sir!

Your humble servant
H.P.

For /
    Mr Sheppard attorney at
       law at Lidcot.
          This.

56. H.P. to Thomas Sheppard

Shalstone,
August the 5th, 1749.

Sir! /

According to promise, I send you seven hare scuts wch. I desire your acceptance of, & wish they may clear your pen to your satisfaction, & am

Your very humble servant
H.P.

P.S. When you do me the favour to come here ab^t. settling the £95 I am to receive, let me have a line when you come, for I am pretty much from home this Astrop season.

For /
    Mr Sheppard attorney at law
       to be left at Mrs Smith's
         at Padbury.
           This.

57. H.P. to Peter Moulson

Shalstone,
August the 13th, 1749.

Sir! /

... The plague of my Shrievalty is almost over, tho' I was sorely fatigued last Buckingham Assizes ...

For /
    Mr Moulson etc ...
       London.

58. H.P. to Thomas Sheppard

Shalstone,
Monday, April the 9th, 1750.

Sir! /

... I accidentally met our High Sheriff at Buckingham who seems desirous to have the Subscription Book but I had it not there, but desire you will write a proper receipt & send it to Mr Wallbank's at Buckingham, &, on the Sheriff's signing it in my presence, I am ready to deliver the book.

I hope I shall have my quietus some time in Trinity Term, & shall be very glad to see you here, & am

Your very humble serv^{t.}
H.P.

For /
    Mr Sheppard attorney at law
        at Lidcot /
            This.

Appendix

LIST OF SUBSCRIBERS TO SHERIFF'S FUND
TAKEN 27 JULY 1749

To the bare list of names which follows the present editor has added the name of each parish of residence, where the identity of the person was fairly certain, and the year in which he served the office of sheriff.

	Name	Remarks	Date of Shrievalty
1	S^{r.} Wm. Bowyer	Denham	
2	George Denton	Hillesden	
3	S^{r.} Wm. Stanhope	Eythrope	
4	Thomas Kensey	Chilton	1746
5	John Wilks	Aylesbury	1754
6	Richard Lowndes	Winslow	1737
7	William Drake	Amersham	
8	Thomas Hill	(?) Little Kimble	
9	John Adams	(?) Swanbourne	
10	William Hayton	Ivinghoe	

	Name	Remarks	Date of Shrievalty
11	Sr. Charles Tyrrell	Thornton	
12	Thomas Willis	Bletchley (son of Browne Willis)	
13	Philip Herbert	Kingsey	
14	Thomas James Selby n.p.	Wavendon	1739
15	Ralph Holt	Loughton	
16	Charles Wodnoth	Maids Moreton	1753
17	Matthias Rogers	(?) Castle Ho, Buckingham	
18	William Basil	(?) Beaconsfield	
19	Thomas Eyre	East Burnham	
20	John Pollard n.p.	Leckhampstead	1735
21	S^{r.} ffrancis Dashwood	West Wycombe	
22	Sr. Thomas Snell	Brill	
23	Sr. Thomas Lee	Hartwell	
24	John Vanhattem	Dinton (see No. 60)	1761
25	Richard Warr	(?) Hughenden	
26	Alex^{r.} Townshend	Thornborough	1750
27	John Wells	Wavendon	
28	John Knap	Little Linford	
29	George Wright n.p.	Gayhurst	
30	Tyringham Backwell	Tyringham	
31	Henry Uthwatt n.p.	Great Linford	1755
32	Henry ffynes n.p.	Wing	
33	Sr. Philip Touchet Chetwood	Chetwode	
34	Thomas Edwards	Terrick, Ellesborough	
35	John Theed	(?) Edlesborough	
36	Humphry Paine		
37	Lester Selman	Chalfont St. Peter	
38	John Robinson	(?) Broughton, or North Crawley	
39	Hugh Barker	Mursley	
40	William Guy n.p.	Marsh Gibbon	
41	Henry Purefoy	Shalstone	1748
42	Anthony Turney	(?) Cublington	
43	Thos. Sheppard	Lidcote (the Under-Sheriff)	
44	John Bristow	Ellesborough	1752

	Name	Remarks	Date of Shrievalty
45	Lancelot Charles Lake	Aston Clinton	
46	Henry Lovebond	Oving	1751
47	John Ansell	Great Missenden	1758
48	Henry Geary		
49	Valentine Knightley	Haversham	
50	John Revett	Chequers, Ellesborough	
51	Richard Smith	Padbury	1724
52	John Warren	(?) Little Marlow	
53	Henry Cooley n.p.	Cheddington	
54	Sr. Charles Palmer	Dorney	
55	Sr. Charles Jones Wake	Hanslope	
56	Sr. Charles Bagot Chester n.p.	Chicheley	
57	David James n.p.	Woughton	
58	Sr. Richard Atkins n.p.	Newport Pagnell	
59	Crail Crail	Britwell Place, Burnham	
60	John Vanhattem n.p.	Dinton (see No. 24)	1761
61	Barn. Backwell	Tyringham	
62	Richd. Greenville	Stowe	
63	George Tash n.p.	Iver	
64	Christopher Towers n.p.	Iver	
65	Richd. Dayrell n.p.	Lillingstone Dayrell	

Additions, Regulations, New Orders & Alterations made to and in the Articles annexed –

At a meeting of the Subscribers the 14th Day of January 1747. It is Resolved that [here follow 51 names out of the 65 quoted] be appointed a Committee and that any five of the said Committee are hereby impowered to make any additions, new orders or Regulations touching the matters contained in the said articles as they shall from Time to Time find necessary.

Resolved that the eleventh clause in the Articles annexed be repealed and instead thereof that any person after the 12th day of ffebruary next and before the first day of November 1748 may become a subscriber to the said articles on payment of five Guineas into the hands of the Treasurer for the time being, to be added to the stock, and that any person whatsoever qualified to serve the office of Sherriff of the county of Bucks and ommitting to become a subscriber before the 1st day of November 1748 shall and may

E

at any time afterwards betwixt the 12th day of ffebruary and the last day of October in any year (except when the office of Sherriff is vacant by Death) be admitted as a Subscriber to the said articles on payment of ten guineas into the hands of the Treasurer for the time being to be added to the Publick Stock, anything in the said articles contained to the contrary notwithstanding.

Resolved that Thomas Hill a subscriber to the annexed articles be appointed Steward for the purposes in the said Articles mentioned.

Resolved that Thomas Sheppard a subscriber be appointed Treasurer and receiver of the subscriptions and is hereby impowered to pay and disburse thereout what shall be necessary for the purposes in the said articles mentioned.

Resolved that the Son of a subscriber to the said Articles shall be admitted to the benfitt of the Subscription on his paying five guineas into the Hands of the Treasurer on or before the first day of November next after his ffarther's Decease.

26th July 1749

Present S^r. W^m. Bowyer, Barron^t., George Denton, Richard Lowndes, Thomas Hill, W^m. Hayton Esquires, & divers other subscribers to the s^d. articles. It being represented by George Tash Esq that Hee & Seuall other Gentlemen of the County of Bucks had not due notice of the s^d. articles so as to become subscribers thereto within the Time thereby limitted for five Guineas It is therefore Resolved for encouraging the said subscription that any Person for the future shall and may become a subscriber to the said Articles on payment of five Guineas into the hands of the Treasurer for the Time being at any time betwixt the twelfth day of ffebruary and the last day of October in any year (except when ye office of Sherriff is vacant by Death) anything in the said Articles or Additions contained to the contrary in any wise notwithstanding.

(b) SOCIAL LIFE

59. H.P. to Rev. Edward Troutbeck

Shalstone,
July the 4th, 1747.

Sir! /

Understanding we have lost our good neighbour Mrs Price, I entreat the favour of you to enquire of some person who attends her funeral if Dr Rayner, a physician of Bath, be living & resident at Bath, and if the small pox is much at Bath or no, and let me know thereof which will oblige

Your humble servant

H.P.

For /

The Rev^{d.} Mr. Troutbeck
   at Westbury.
      This.

60. H.P. to The Cheltenham Postmaster

Shalstone,

April 18th, 1742.

I, having occasion to drink your waters at Cheltenham, am obliged to write to you, the Postmaster, to let me know if the small pox be at Cheltenham. If not, I shall be there soon after I have your answer, wch. I desire you will oblige me with, & am

Your unknown humble servant

H.P.

I have no other opportunity but writing by the post to you, it being across the country.

For /

The Postmaster at the Post Office
   at Cheltenham
      in
         Gloucestershire.

61. H.P. to Thomas Jervoise[1]

Bath,

August the 3^{d.}, 1742.

Sir! /

I am favoured with both your letters & thank you for your kind invitation

---

[1] Thomas Jervoise, of Herriard House near Basingstoke in Hampshire, was Henry Purefoy's first cousin once removed. He was M.P. for Hampshire and other constituencies between 1691 and 1710. His grandson, George Jervoise, was to be Henry Purefoy's heir.

to Herriard, & should have waited on you there before now had not all our servants fell ill of the scarlet fever & sore throat, wch. has been very rife & mortal in our parts. It detained us at home so long, that I despair of waiting on you this, for we are ordered to drink these waters six weeks & by that time I am afraid the roads will be bad, but we hope next spring or the first fine season to do ourselves the pleasure of visiting you at Herriard. My mother & self both join in our love & service to yourself & family, & I am Sir!

Your affect. kinsman &
very humble servant.
H.P.

P.S. Now the season is so fine, should be glad to see you here or else to hear of your health, & pray direct for me at Major Bolton's at Bath, in Somersetshire by way of London. Your kinsman & old acquaintance S^r. Hugh Clopton is here.

62. H.P. to the Rev. Richard Dalby

Shalstone,
September the 8th, 1736.

Sir! /

I am favoured with yours of the 12th August last. I am glad you concluded your journey safe, & that your preferment is like to prove to your mind, & hope this will find you perfectly recovered of your fever, but, if it should not, I am informed there is an excellent medicinal spring at a place called Saint Landulphs in your County of Cornwall, partly of the same nature with Scarborough Spa waters; probably if you were to drink this Landulph water for a month or so, it might restore your constitution to a due temper, & for the future fortify you against any noxious particles that may arise from the tin or copper mines & so mix with the air. As to any vapours that arise from the sea, I don't believe they will hurt you for I have been at Bristol where there then was as foggy & thick an air as well could be & it was occasioned by vapours arising from the sea, but I felt no ill effects from it so must attribute your disorders to the effluvia of the mines. Don't be sollicitous about the gelding. He proves extremely well. I have no news to send you, but our town of Buckingham is grievously visited with the small pox, the last I heard of it, it was in three score houses, so forasmuch as it is so universal hope it will soon be over. I thank God our Shalstone folks have escaped it hitherto. There never was so great a scarcity of hares as with us at present & but a few partridge & pheasants. This last season at Astrop Wells has afforded more diversion than usual, & there has been much dancing & pleasantry there among the young folks. Myself & the rest of your friends here are heartily glad that we are like as to have you among us next summer, & that you are so good as to think of us tho' at so great a distance, & when you come into these parts of the world, I assure you no one of your friends will have more satisfaction in seeing you than, Sir! /

Your affect: friend & ĥle serv^{t.}

H.P.

P.S. / My mother joins with me in our service & respect & shall be glad to hear of your health & success in your school.

For / The Rev^{d.} Mr. Dalby
    at Helston in Cornwall
    By way of London.

63. H.P. to Samuel Pashler

Shalstone,
October the 21st, 1752.

Sir! /

I have considered further of the affair you was mentioning to me, and as I live 3 miles from Buckingham it will be impossible for me to act as a Justice for your Corporation on account of my ill state of health, so there will be no occasion for me to wait on my Lord on Tuesday.

Shall be glad to wait on you & Mr Wallbank & Miss Barrett here whenever your leisure will permit, & with our compliments to you all, am Sir!

Your very humble serv^{t.}

H.P.

For /
    Mr Pashler at
      Buckingham.
      This.

64. H.P. to the Rev. Dr. Bowles

Shalstone,
August the 15th, 1750.

Sir! /

We propose to go to Astrop[1] on Friday morning next, & hope for your good company's, having two places in the coach for you. Shall call on you about 8 o'clock, & with our compliments to you all, I am in haste, Sir! /

Your very humble serv^{t.}
H.P.

For /

The Rev^{d.} Dr. Bowles
   at Brackley.
     This.

65. E.P. to Catharine Willis

Shalstone,
May the 28th, 1748.

This is to acquaint Miss Catharine Willis that I expect to go from home very suddenly, so can have no thoughts of waiting on you to Lord Cobham's Gardens,[2] and give you this trouble that you might not be disappointed. My son joins me in our compliments to yourself & all your family, & I am

Your humble servant
E.P.

For /

Miss Catharine Willis at Brown
   Willis's Esq. at Whaddon Hall.
     This.

---

1 Astrop is situated some five miles to the south-west of Banbury. The medicinal qualities of its spring were discovered in the late seventeenth century, and, by 1750, it had become a social centre of some significance. Gambling, dancing and conversational facilities were provided for those coming to take the waters, and, although clearly no rival to Bath or Cheltenham, the Astrop season was something that county families like the Purefoys would be loath to miss.

2 At Stowe House: these famous gardens, providing one of the best examples of eighteenth-century landscaping, were laid out by Richard Temple, 1st Viscount Cobham. 'Capability' Brown began his career as a gardener in the kitchen garden at Stowe.

66. H.P. to Francis Fell

Shalstone,
July the 7th, 1751.

M[r] Fell /

I desire you will come over here as soon as may be to take measure on me for a suit of second mourning & to bring patterns of clothe with you. I must have them made and brought for me to wear on next Monday come se'nnight at night being the 15th of this instant July, for next morning early being the 16th, I am warned to be on the Grand Jury. You should have known sooner but I did not know myself till last night that I was to be at the Assize. Pray let the patterns be fine fast clothe . . .

Your friend to serve you
H.P.

For /

M[r] Francis Fell
a Taylor at Chipping Norton
in Oxfordshire.
By London.

67. E.P. to the Rev. Dr. David Trimnell[1]

Shalstone,
Octob[r] the 4th, 1747.

Sir! /

I am favoured with yours dated the 19th of last month, & am much obliged to you for your kind invitation to Lincoln, but the winter comes on so fast that we durst not afford ourselves the pleasure of waiting on you there, but if you should come into this country before the Astrop Season we shall be proud to wait on you & your family at Shalstone. Since I had the favour of seeing you last, my son has had the jaundice & he was so bad with it [that] I was afraid I should have lost him, but I thank God now he is somewhat recovered. We are obliged to you for your good intentions, but

---

1 David Trimnell (1675–1756) came from a well-endowed clerical family. He was appointed Archdeacon of Leicester in 1716 and Precentor of Lincoln Cathedral in 1718. He appeared regularly at Astrop and at the Buckingham Assizes.

the match you propose is in no ways agreeable. Pray make our compliments acceptable to M^rs. Trimnell & Miss & accept the same from Sir!

Your very humble servant
E.P.

For /

    The Rev^d. D^r. Trimnell
       at Lincoln.
    By way of London.

68. H.P. to Samuel Passelow

Shalstone,
Octob: the 4th, 1746.

Sir! /

I shall let down my fish pond on Tuesday morning next, & entreat the favour of your company about 10 o'clock. Pray don't mention the fishing to anybody. My mother joins with me in our compliments to self & Mr Wallbank & Miss Barrett, & I am Sir!

Your humble servant
H.P.

For /

    Mr Passelow at M^r. Wallbank's
       at Buckingham.
          This.

69. H.P. to Risley Risley

Shalstone,
August the 10th, 1746.

Sir! /

I am summoned on the Grand Jury, but since that have an unexpected call to Northampton, but shall return home by Thursday night. I must entreat the favour of you to make my excuse to the judge (when I am called over) for my non-attendance, wch. will much oblige

Your most humble servant
H.P.

P.S. Our compliments attend yourself & Mrs Risley & Mrs Hook, & hope
for the favour of your company's at Shalstone soon.

For /
    Risley Risley Esq.
        at Chetwood /
           This.

70. E.P. to Harry Wallbank

Shalstone,
June the 17th, 1745.

Sir! /

    My son being one of the Commissioners ab^t· the Charity[1] at Gawcot
attends at the Crosskeys on Wednesday next, & if it agreeable to you &
Miss Bett. I will take a commons with you on that day, & be with you
between one or two o'clock. Let me know by the bearer if you are not
otherwise engaged. Our compliments attend you all, & I am

Your humble serv^t·
E.P.

For /
    M^r· Wallbank a Surgeon
        at Buckingham.
           This.

71. H.P. to John Wentworth Cresswell

Shalstone,
8th Septembr·, 1744.

Sir! /

    I am informed the Way of the World[2] will be acted this night at West-
bury. It is to begin about half [an] hour after 5 o'clock. I hope we shall have

---

1 A charity established under the will of Sir Simon Benett, by which £20 was annually
to be distributed to the poor of Buckingham.

2 The Purefoys seem to have attended plays once a year. Apart from the Congreve
masterpiece mentioned here, we know that some of Shakespeare's tragedies were also
performed. They appear to have been held under the auspices of Mr Price of Westbury.

the favour of your companies to drink a dish of tea, & then to wait on you thither.

Our compliments attend you both & I am Sir!

Your very humble servant
H.P.

For /

John Wentworth Cresswell Esq.
at Lillingston Lovell.
This.

72. E.P. to Mrs Wallbank

Shalstone,
July the 13th, 1743.

If it is agreeable to Mrs Wallbank & she is not otherwise engaged, I will come & dine with her on Tuesday next, being the Buckingham Assize.

And if it so, I desire you will give me leave to bring some of my chickens & bacon etc, and favour me with your answer by the post boy, who brings our news on Friday next. Our compliments attend Mr Wallbank & yourself & Miss, and I am

Your humble servant
E.P.

For /

Mrs Wallbank at
Buckingham.
This.

73. E.P. to Mrs Susan Price

Shalstone,
Novemb^r. 11th, 1738.

Dear Sukey /

We were coming yesterday to Whitfield in hopes to wait on M^r. & M^rs. Price, but were prevented of the pleasure of seeing you all by reason the axtree of the chariot broke in Westbury field, so we were forced to send for the coach to have us home. We thank God no other harm happened to us. This accident will hinder our coming to you this moon, so hope we shall see some of your family here soon. I had the 3 couple of chickens & have ordered the bearer to pay you 3 shillings. I have ordered the bearer to go to Radson for a pig if you think it is not gone. We both join in service & respect to Mr Price & all the family, & I am

Your affect: Godmother
E.P.

For /

    Mrs Susan Price

        at Whitfield

        This.

P.S. My dairy maid is very sickly & goes away, if you hear of ever an one pray let me know.

74. H.P. to Rev. William Price

Shalstone,
Wednesday, October the 25th, 1738.

Sir! /

Yesterday I fished a pond & I think you mentioned some time ago you had occasion for some store fish, wch. if you have, if you would send your servant over tomorrow morning with things to carry 'em in, I shall have about 100 brace of store carp at your service. My mother & self join in our service & respect to yourself & family, & I am Sir!

Your very ĥle serv^t
H.P.

For /

    The Rev^{d.} Mr. Price

        at Whitfield

        This.

75. H.P. to Peter Moulson

Shalstone,
February the 25th, 1740.

Sir! /

I send you enclosed my lottery ticket which I desire you will sell for me, for after the 15th of this next March, as I am informed, they won't be accepted; be so good to keep the money for it till further orders. We received your kind present of oysters & sturgeon, w^ch· were exceedingly good. We return you our hearty [thanks] for them.

The following tragedy is true. On Saturday last, the Rev^d· M^r· Burton of Brackley in Northtonshire, his servant man being saucy, he ordered him to leave his service; instead of that he went to work in the barn amongst the rest of the workmen. Mr Burton coming soon after into the barn, he spoke to him & bad him go of[f] from his ground, w^ch· the fellow refusing to do in saucy manner, Mr Burton stroke him over the back with his cane, on which the fellow upped with a long fork he had in his hand, & stroke Mr Burton a blow on the side of his head w^ch· felled him down, & after a groan or two he instantly died. The servants who were by, whilst one held Mr Burton up and the other run for a surgeon, the fellow who murdered him made his escape & is not yet taken.

This clergyman was a man of as good parts & learning as most in our country, & his death is much lamented, S^r· Thos· Abney the Council married his sister.

My mother & self join in our respects & services to yourself & Miss Moulson, & I am with due esteem, Sir!

Your very hle servant
H.P.

For /

Mr Moulson . . .
London.

P.S. As the rascal made of[f], he, meeting a servant boy of Mr Burton's, he told him he had laid his master in his long sleep & gloried in the wicked fact. Pray favour me with a line or two that the ticket is come safe to you and sold.

76. H.P. to Browne Willis[1]

Shalstone,
February 2^d·, 1750.

Sir! /

I am heartily sorry to hear you are indisposed with a cold & wish your speedy recovery, for it should please God to take you from us, the loss of

---

[1] This is merely one of several letters from Henry Purefoy to Browne Willis, the antiquarian, in which information about the county and its families was passed on. In such a narrowly-defined community, the origins of neighbours, their wealth and political history, were obviously matters of great interest, and the source of endless comparison and speculation.

you would be very sensibly felt. I return many thanks for the sketch of your History of Bucks you sent me to look over, & as to Mr. Minshull's affair, Mr Francis Garvan of the Inner Temple in the year 1720 told me that Dick Minshull the horse racer, presently after the Peace of Ryswick, sent a set of fine horses down to Dover to be exported to St. Germains as a present to the late King James the Second, but the then officers of the port of Dover, getting intelligence that Minshull was a Papist, seized these horses for the government's use, they being above the value of £5. This disappointm^{t.} piqued Minshull so far that he declared he would have as fine horses as any man in England for all the government, & immediately set upon breeding & running race horses, & this unhappy branch of conduct he used to lament & acknowledge was the occasion & rise of all his future misfortunes, for I never heard he was gamester either at cards or dice. As to Mr Garvan, he was a Catholic gentleman & I was favoured with his friendship & acquaintance. He was a very polite gentleman, & a man of veracity & much admired & esteemed by late Ld. North & Grey & the Visc^{t.} Montague of Sussex as well as by everybody who knew him, & I have been at his Chambers in 1720; they were near the Cloisters in the Inner Temple. His home was in the County of Clare in Ireland & his estate there reckoned about £1,000 a year. This I mention if you should have further curiosity to enquire after Minshull, for Garvan knew him as much of him in his decline of life as anybody.

As to my own family, my great grandfather George Purefoy kept two coaches & six horses at Wadley in Berks, & fed the neighbouring poor in so plentiful a manner at his porter's lodge, that at night his servants have brought him two basons full of the twigs of birch brooms to him, every twig denoting a person who reced his alms, that he might know next time what quantity of victuals to provide for them, in so grand & hospitable a manner did he live.

As to Francis Ingolsby (the eldest son of Sir Richard) who was member in the Rump Parliament, his first estate at Lenborough was entailed, & my mother says when she first came into this county there was a strong report of the barbarity of this Francis Ingolsby & his wife in setting up a pack of dogs & maintaining a fine set of hunting horses to draw in his eldest son to cut of[f] the entail of the estate at Lemborough, wch. attempt succeeded & thereon the ruin of that family.

As to Sir George Moor of Maids Moreton, he was created a Bar^{t.} 26th July 1665, & as I imagine passed over his estate there to Dr. Bate Physician to Oliver Cromwell & King Charles the 2^{d.}, whose son Justice Bates enjoyed the same after him, & to whose person and merit and good character you cannot be a stranger to. My mother says when she was a child & at Mr Fish her uncle's at Bellbar near Hatfield in Hertfordshire, there was one Sir George Moore, who hired a seat in a lane by Northall Common & had 19 children followed him & his lady to church there, & she thinks this S^r· George Moore might be the person.

We are very much obliged to you for your kind intentions of giving us your company here, & hope the ways will permit for us to see you here soon, & with our compliments I am Sir! very respectfully

Your most humble servant
H.P.

P.S. S^r· Richard Ingolsby of Wallridge who signed the death warrant etc was made a Kn^t· of the Bath at [the] Coronation of King Charles the 2^d·

For /
    Brown Willis Esq
        D^r· of Laws at his
            seat at Whaddon.
                To be left at the Cross Keys
                  Inn at Buckingham
                    This.

3

The Estate

A SQUIRE'S relationship with his estate was as intimate as the affectionate bond which he might hold with a near relation. Ownership allowed him that position in parish and shire which has been discussed earlier. Possession guaranteed a continuing link between the Purefoy generations, past, present and future. It was a duty on each incumbent to maintain the economic efficiency of the estate and to improve its yield. At the same time, since the financial contract between landlord and tenant lay at the bottom of the local politics described in Chapter One, it was also important to preserve harmony in this sphere as consistently as possible. A nice balance of these two considerations marked the prosperous and popular squire.

As Letters 77 to 87 indicate, estate ownership involved continual effort with regard to neighbours and possible purchasers of agricultural produce. If fences had to be repaired, rivers cleaned or contracts honoured, a barrage of ever-increasing threats might be necessary to keep other people up to the mark. Few people in the eighteenth century had any objection to threatening legal action. Indeed a good law-suit might even be entertaining, if well argued. And should the courts prove to be too expensive, the litigants could have recourse to arguing their cases before two referees, one being chosen by each side. Most local disputes could be settled in this way, and in all of them the opinion of the oldest inhabitants of the village would normally prove decisive (Letters 107 and 108). When in doubt, the eighteenth century always fell back to the safety of customary practice. From time to time it was thought important to restate traditional usages, in case their authority should be weakened by apparently falling into disuse.

Much the same considerations affected relations between landlord and tenant (Letters 88 to 109). They invariably involved some compromise between a jealous guardianship of traditional rights and concessions to a difficult economic situation. For example, it would be wrong to be misled by the numerous cases of distraint which are referred to in the letters. Quite clearly, Henry Purefoy was an efficient landlord, who demanded that his rent be paid on time and who readily sent the bailiffs in when arrears became too painful. But since good, sober and honest tenants were hard to find in the stagnant agricultural situation in the first half of the century, a certain amount of latitude had to be given. The diaries record that a certain Edward May's goods were distrained for rent in 1729, but, since the same thing happened nine years later, the process cannot have involved total ruin. The taking up of references by landowners (Letter 102) is a further example of the difficulty of their position. Rather than lose a normally reliable tenant, or, worse still, have a farm standing untenanted, land-owners would prefer to remit rent and wait for better times. The May family was still living in Shalstone at least as late as 1805.

Examples could be multiplied of this curious symbiosis between tenant and landlord, which formed the backbone of English agriculture. The account books at Shalstone give details of what were very obviously medi-eval taxes in kind that were still to be paid in Henry Purefoy's time. At Christmas time Goodman Simkins paid '2 couple of pullets'. Goodman Penell did the same with the addition of 'a couple of fat cock turkeys'. On the other hand, the same sources suggest that a good tenant could expect prompt repairs and an ungrudging response to his needs. On the 23 December 1746, Henry Purefoy noted that 'Goodman Wm. May junior of Shalstone had 2 gate posts, twelve rails, 2 heads & 2 soles, for 2 gates that part his yard'. The severe tone of some of the following letters should therefore be treated with caution. Economic power did not lie exclusively with landlords in this period. A hint of resignation on the part of a reliable tenant farmer brought the relationship very quickly into balance.

Much more difficult in a way was the Purefoy connection with the rural craftsmen, who had to be called in from time to time for repairs of a specialist kind (Letters 110 to 121). Normally, one stone-mason or well-digger would service several parishes as a self-employed expert. This kind of labour, however, was highly irregular and undisciplined. All kinds of agricultural labour was highly seasonal, with frenzied bouts of harvesting or sowing interspersed with long periods of enforced or chosen idleness. As these letters suggest, this tradition with the rural craftsmen was just as strong. A natural disinclination to proceed with a job was reinforced by the problem of co-ordinating the availability of materials and labour, the vagaries of the weather, and the discomfort of travelling even small distances. Even so, the Charles Parker referred to in the letters seems to have performed his rôle of stone-mason without any sense of urgency or responsibility. Such men could not be easily threatened, as they would in all probability have a monopoly of their craft in their district. In this pre-industrial community, skilled labour could not be hurried, and the Purefoys, like any other prospective employer, simply had to exercise restraint.

What emerges from these examples is the fact that county society in the eighteenth century ran on a very subtle system of checks and balances. Simply because squires, as landowners, were unchallenged in their management of local justice or national politics did not mean that the lower orders in the countryside had no means of redress. As long as good tenants were hard to find, as long as one landlord poached good farmers away from his neighbour, or as long as the skills of the rural craftsmen were scarce and in demand, the system would always be modified in favour of these groups. Their methods of exerting influence were far less formal and legally defined than the squire's, but they were almost as effective.

(a) THE PUREFOYS AND THEIR NEIGHBOURS

77. H.P. to Mrs James

Shalstone,
Sunday, June 27th, 1736.

Madam /

My mother & self thought to have had the favour of seeing you here before this, that I might have had an opportunity of telling you that the jury, who sat on the body of our servant who was lately drowned, have threatened to indict the farther ford at Huntmill between you & me, unless there is a rail put up to prevent any body tumbling in again – it must be done when the water is low & I shall speedily set a workman to do my part – & I thought it necessary to acquaint you that you might at the same time set on a man on your part & then it will be the less trouble – if it should be indicted & the indictment once filed, it cannot be taken off again under

F

expence & on the oath of two credible witnesses. My mother's & my service & respect waits on you & I am, Madam,

Your very humble serv^t

H.P.

For / Mrs James at
    Finmere
      This.

78. H.P. to James Perkins

Shalstone,
April the 15th, 1737.

Mr Perkins /

Your tenant Enox tells me he is to repair the rails on his side by Potford, & that you are to find rough timber & he workmanship, and that as yet you have not let him have wood to repair it. This he told me yesterday.

My mother has now 19 ewes & lambs go in the Lower Rinehill next Potford, and, it being next the high road, until you repair the rails they will be constantly in danger of straying away, so I don't doubt but you will be so good a neighbour as to order the tenant wood forthwith to repair it, which will oblige

Your friend & serv^t

H.P.

For /
    Mr James Perkins
      at Tingewick /
        This.

79. E.P. to Mrs Anne Warr

Shalstone,
Decemb^r the 3^d, 1737.

Mrs Warr /

I rece'd your letter & admire you should choose me of all your customers to make a fool on.

I do assure you if you don't pay the bearer hereof, John Buckingham,

£3 14s. 6d. I will order you to be sued forthwith, and if you refuse to take the fourteen pounds of butter I send this day at 6ᵈ a pound, I have ordered my servant to sell it in the market, & if it fails to fetch 6ᵈ a pound you must up the deficiency to

E.P.

For /

    Mʳˢ Anne Warr
        at Buckingham
           This.

P.S. I have sent you sixteen pound of butter you ordered to be salted, which is included in the £3 14s. 6d.

80. E.P. to John Lucas

Shalstone,
Decembʳ the 29ᵗʰ, 1737.

This is to desire Mʳ Lucas to let me know the circumstances of Goodman Isaac Sheppard of your town – I am told he is rent run & that he will be seized for rent. I desire you will let me know if there is anything in it by reason I have eight heifers there at straw. This remains a secret to me, for I have never spoke of it till now. I apply myself to you to inform me of the truth. Your answer by the bearer, if not with convenience, leave it at home & I will send a servant for it tomorrow. My son joins with me in service to you & Mʳˢ Lucas, & I am

Your humble servᵗ·
E.P.

For /

    Mʳ John Lucas
        at Westbury /
           This.

81. H.P. to Conquest Jones

Shalstone,
February the 28ᵗʰ, 1738.

Mʳ Jones /

    According to your desire, I have spoke to Mʳ Hunt the baker, & he tells me that Flowers warranted the mare to him to be sound at the time he bought her & that she would stand at house; so soon as ever he brought her home & kept her in the stable, she broke out with the mange & that was the reason he says she was kept at grass as a distempered mare so long before he had her . . . if you'll take the mare again, Mr Hunt says he is willing to give you a guinea with her or else to pay you three pounds by a Lady day next – And I believe that is as much as he is able to do – He seems concerned you should intend to arrest him, or else I believe I could not have prevailed on him to do what he now proposes – if you were to arrest him, there will be nothing for you, for I must have my years rent first and then if I was to seize I verily believe there will be no overplus – if you will let me have your answer, I will endeavour to get the money for you against you come down at Lady day next, & am

Your humble servant
H.P.

For /
     Mr Conquest Jones at his house
        the next door to the Angel
           Inn in Piccadilly.
           London.

82. H.P. to Jemmy Paine

Shalstone,
March the 14th, 1738.

Mr Paine /

The tenants complain of your cuts of furze you bought standing in the Cowpasture (which if cut down it would be the better for their cattle now the grass begins to grow), so I desire you would have them cut down forthwith & get off the ground as soon as may be, which will oblige

Your humble serv^t
H.P.

For /
     Mr Jemmy Paine a Baker
        at Brackley.

P.S. If you don't take the furze away you will be the loser, for I have
     promised them the ground shall be rid.

83. H.P. to John Lucas

Shalstone,
Wednesday, March the 26th, 1740.

Mr Lucas /

I have not seen you here according to appointm^t, [and] must tell you of the information I have rece^d since I saw you.

Eight years ago, I cleaned the mill dam at Huntmill, & then the workmen (who are now living) carried the mud taken out of the dam on my land & when Old Savage rented Huntmill my mother cleaned it & laid it on likewise, &, when there was a dispute about the island at Huntmill, Mr Bly told me the river was mine as far as the mill dam extended, & now I understand all mill dams are originally dug out of the owner's land. Therefore desire you will inform Thomas Yates either to deliver me the mud again or else to make me satisfaction for it before Wednesday next, otherwise shall be obliged to proceed against him according to law.

I am your h^le servant
H.P.

For /
Mr John Lucas
This.

84. H.P. to Mr Morgan

Shalstone,
August 22th, 1741.

Mr Morgan /

I am sorry to tell you my servants & workmen have cut one of your oaks instead of my own. It is not used, & I should be glad if you would come or send somebody to see it, that I make recompense for their misdoings. I understand it to be yours but as yesterday – if you have a mind I should have it, if you chose one man & I another what they two decide I will stand to.[1] I have not cut a tree down at this time of year but for a beam to lay a parlour floor upon, & I sent them to choose one of the most mazzardly[2] sticks & the least lop because of the bark. I hear the lop of this oak will throw out about a score of fagots and a small matter of hard wood. I hear

---

1 This recourse to unofficial arbitration, with each of the disputants appointing one referee, was a favourite device for settling disputes.
2 Mazzardly: dialect word meaning knotty or knarled.

your son comes to Buckingham fair tomorrow. Should be glad if he would call here & stay all night, & then he may judge of the affair. My mother's & my service & respect is with yourself & family & I am in haste

Your humble serv^t

H.P.

For /

Mr Morgan senior at

Lee

This.

85. H.P. to Richard Shillingford

Shalstone,

Monday, May the 28th, 1744.

Mr Shillingford /

Goodwi: Salmon came to me yesterday with a complaint that you refuse to pay her husband for felling the oaks, and that you have paid Gascoign five & forty shillings & that you should say as I set Salmon to work I must pay him. I have promised to give Salmon an answer by next Saturday, & desire you will come here & explain yourself or else do it by letter, wch. you may send any night by Goodman Gurnet who works here. As you took the money for felling the trees you must pay the workmen. I am

Your humble servant

H.P.

For / Mr Shillingford a joiner

at Buckingham

This.

86. E.P. to H. Wallbank

Shalstone,

April the 8th, 1747.

Sir! /

I send you enclosed a notice which I desire you will deliver on my behalf to the Collector & other Officers of the Excise, & ask them when I must pay the money, & if my carriage should not be marked before I pay my duty for it, & if there is any body authorized to receive the money &

[if] it is proper to pay it before the carriage is marked. I desire you will pay the four pounds for me & take a receipt for it, & I will either bring it or send it you in 2 or 3 days time if I don't see you here before that. This will much oblige

Your humble servant
E.P.

P.S. Our compliments attend you all.

For /

    Mʳ Wallbank at
        Buckingham /
            This.

To the Collectors & other Officers of the Excise at Buckingham in the County of Bucks.

Gentlemen /

This gives you notice that I, Elizabeth Purefoy, widow, keep a carriage with four wheels & am ready to pay the duty for the same, when I know you are the persons authorized to receive it, and that the parish or the place where I reside at is Shalstone near this our County Town of Buckingham, & I desire to know whether the carriage I pay duty for must not be marked before I pay the money. I am, Gentlemen,

Your humble servant
E.P.

87. H.P. to James Perkins

Shalstone,
September 14ᵗʰ, 1748.

Mʳ· Perkins /

The season for cleaning rivers [here?] & springs being very low, I think it proper for cleaning those against the Hunney Holmes & desire you will give orders to clean your side & I will do the like. I am

Your friend & servant
H.P.

For /

    Mʳ James Perkins at
        Tingewick
            This.

(*b*) THE PUREFOYS AND THEIR TENANTS

88. H.P. to Edward Baylis

Shalstone,
Sunday, 29th Feb^{ry}, 1735.

Mr Baylis /

Tom Penell tells me that you said this morning that you would rent the ground Mr. Hodgkinson now rents.

It is not as yet set[1] & you may rent it at the same rent Mr Hodgkinson now does, wch is £9 a year to enter at Lady Day next. I do not think the house Simkins lives in & Dawes Close would be any service to Goodwi: Penell, 'twould be so much charge to keep it in repair & I shall never let it be set for a poor body to live in. Let me see you here some time within this 2 or 3 days in a morning. Then I shall be sure to be at home, & am

Your h͡le serv^t.
H.P.

To Mr Edwd. Baylis a
stonemason at Helmdon /
   This.

89. H.P. to Master Jones

Shalstone,
May 28th, 1736.

Master Jones /

You have been so often heard to say you would come to live at Shalstone again if I had anything to set. William Hobcraft leaves his bargain[2] next Lady Day. I thought I could do no less than let you have the refusal of the bargain if your mind is not altered. Your answer will oblige

Your friend to serve you
H.P.

My mother's & my service
is with your wife & self
For / Goodman John Jones
   at Wappenham. This d.

---

[1] Set: let or leased.
[2] Bargain: the word Henry Purefoy always uses for tenancy.

90. H.P. to John Greaves

Shalstone,
Saturday, August 7th, 1736.

M[r] Greaves /

You talked of selling your crop to my mother in order thereto she got somebody to look on it.

Your mind I find is altered, for you have ordered it to be cut – I shall not be willing it should go off the ground, so desire you will call here sometime between this & Wednesday next – You can't be ignorant of the covenant in the lease whereby it is covenanted all the stuff is to be spent on the premises – I am

Your friend to serve you
H.P.

For /
M[r] John Greaves
    at Padbury. This d.

91. H.P. to the Rev. Richard Dalby

Shalstone,
February the 14th, 1737.

Sir ! /

I rece'd yours of the 1st instant & am sorry to hear you have no better state of health, & do assure you nobody wishes your recovery of that valuable blessing more than myself. And as to the person whom my mother & self at present wish to see well settled in the Rectory in case of an avoidance, I believe you cannot be altogether a stranger to him. However bare promises before hand only will not do, you know how we have been served in the affair already. As to M[r] Townsend, he has set my tenants tithe to an out town man, & permits M[r] Tayler's tenants to take their tithe at two shillings in the pound notwithstanding the greatest part of their land is ploughed & broke up. His ingratitude is enough to make anybody look about them. As to good brandy or good French wine, if it can be got safe to Shalstone,[1] it will be acceptable & we will pay you for it with thanks. I am glad to hear

---

[1] The spirits are quite likely to have been smuggled into Cornwall, thereby evading very severe Customs duties.

your school increases & wish your health may do the same, & with my mother's blessing & my service to you I am

Your very humble serv^t

H.P.

For /

    The Revd. Mr Dalby at
       Helston in Cornwall
    By London.

92. E.P. to Thomas Robotham

Shalstone,
May the 1st, 1737.

I am forced to give Mr Robotham this trouble, having been called on for some quit rent which is to be paid in cummin seed[1] – so pray send me seven pounds of cummin seed done up in single pounds, you are to have it at the drugsters. Send it with the rest of the things & let us know the newest fashioned hats the ladies wear. My son & self join in our service & respect to you & Mrs Robotham, & I am

Your humble servant.

E.P.

For /

    Mr Robotham at the Kings head
       at Islington near London.

P.S. The small pox is broke out again here at John Hobcrafts.

93. H.P. to Goodwife Meaks

Shalstone,
April the 11th, 1739.

Goodwi: Meaks /

    I understand you have administered to your late husband. There is

---

1 The rent was paid to the Withers family for farming Huntmill. Cummin seed was an inferior kind of pepper grown in Europe as a meat preservative. The nature of this quit rent had clearly been fixed in the Middle Ages when this kind of commodity was highly prized.

twenty shillings in arrear for rent, which I desire you to bring forthwith &
let me know when by the bearer, which will prevent any trouble from

Yours in haste
H.P.

For / Goodwi: Meaks
   This d.

94. H.P. to John Welchman

Shalstone,
Novemb^r the 30th, 1739.

Sir! /

Mr Hunt's notice was delivered to him himself on Monday last by the
bearer hereof in Hunt's stable in his yard & within ten yards of the dwelling
house, we don't pretend to seize anything of Hunt's but what is without
doors or in the barns or stables. Young William May's notice was delivered
to him himself on Monday last in the Close called Daws Close, wch he rents
of me by the said William Baker. This Daw's Close is about half a mile from
the farm house the s^{d.} William May rents. I hope both these notices will
stand good, which pray let me know by the bearer for he is the person that
delivered them. I am in haste

Your hte serv^t
H.P.

For /
   Mr Welchman sen^r
      attorney at law at Brackley
      This.

95. H.P. to John Welchman

Shalstone,
Saturday, Decemb^r the 1st, 1739.

Sir! /

When I was with you last, something happened that when I asked you
abt my distraining part of my tenant Wm. May's cattle between 5 & 6 at

twenty shillings in arrear for rent, which I desire you to bring forthwith &
let me know when by the bearer, which will prevent any trouble from

Yours in haste
H.P.

For / Goodwi: Meaks
This d.

94. H.P. to John Welchman

Shalstone,
Novemb[r] the 30th, 1739.

Sir! /

M[r] Hunt's notice was delivered to him himself on Monday last by the
bearer hereof in Hunt's stable in his yard & within ten yards of the dwelling
house, we don't pretend to seize anything of Hunt's but what is without
doors or in the barns or stables. Young William May's notice was delivered
to him himself on Monday last in the Close called Daws Close, w[ch] he rents
of me by the said William Baker. This Daw's Close is about half a mile from
the farm house the s[d.] William May rents. I hope both these notices will
stand good, which pray let me know by the bearer for he is the person that
delivered them. I am in haste

Your h[t]e serv[t]
H.P.

For /
M[r] Welchman sen[r]
attorney at law at Brackley
This.

95. H.P. to John Welchman

Shalstone,
Saturday, Decemb[r] the 1[st], 1739.

Sir! /

When I was with you last, something happened that when I asked you
abt my distraining part of my tenant Wm. May's cattle between 5 & 6 at

night, it was after sunset & you did not give me so full an answer thereto as
I could have wished.

These cattle which were 8 cows were in Daws Close, but when I had
seized the other cattle by daylight & had drove them home, – Will. May
meeting me attempted to drive off the cattle in Daws Close, wch he was
prevented doing (as he confessed before witness) by the sudden return back
of the bearer whom Will: May helped afterwards to drive these 8 cows
home & help to brand them himself. I hope the distress of these last 8 cows
is good tho' about an hour after sunset.

Your answer by the bearer will oblige

Your humble serv^t

H.P.

For /

    Mr Welchman senior
       attorney at law at Brackley
       This.

96. H.P. to William Jelly.

Shalstone,
Dec^r· the 8th, 1739.

William Jelly /

Goodwi: Penell having sold you some sheep, pigs and calves on my
account, I understand you have not paid the money for them.

This acquaints you, if you do not send the money by young George
Penell the bearer hereof, I shall order my lawyer to proceed against you,
which that you would prevent by paying the money is the desire of

H.P.

For /

    Mr William Jelly a
       Butcher at Buckingham
       This.

97. H.P. to John Welchman

Shalstone
Dec^r· the 19th, 1739.

Sir! /

I desire you will come over here the Thursday after X^tmas day about

10 o'clock to keep my Court,[1] & let me know as much by the bearer & I
will endeavour to get the people to attend then. Pray send the articles by
the bearer & do them up in a piece of paper & give him a charge they are
not wetted. I am Sir!

Your humble Serv[t]
H.P.

For /

    M[r] Welchman sen[r.] Attorney
      at Law at Brackley /
        This.

12. March 1750.   'paid M[r] John Land (Attorney at Law) for keeping my
                  Co[t] Baron & in full in presence of my Mother Purefoy
                  £1 1. 0.'

98. H.P. to Conquest Jones

Shalstone,
Sunday June 8th, 1740.

Sir! /

    I am importuned by Hunt the baker's family, (whom I believe to be
much honester than himself), to give you this trouble, to know if you would
be so good as to accept seven pounds in satisfaction for your debt and
charges – I myself & the rest of the creditors are willing to comply, tho'
for my own part I shall be a twenty pound loser by him, which indeed I
could compel old M[r] Hunt to pay, but he has been so great a loser by his
extravagant son that he has scarce left enough to buy himself and his wife
bread. If you don't comply, young Hunt must run the country, if you please
to accept of this seven pounds on the terms above you may be assured of
that money. Your answer will oblige

Your humble servant
H.P.

For /

    M[r] Conquest Jones next door to the
    Angel Inn in Piccadilly. London.

---

[1] Certain landowners had been given the right in the Middle Ages of holding a Court
within their own parishes, in which to settle disputes between parishioners or tenants.
A lawyer would normally be employed to ensure that the strict provisions of the law
were not infringed.

99. H.P. to John Welchman

Shalstone,
Sept^r· the 10th, 1740.

Sir! /

The Sheriff's officer Mr Hall has William Hunt in hold & if you should have him to gaol I believe you will never have a farthing. But he informs me he has two wagons, one whereof my mother bad six pounds for, & the other they value at five, & that he has some old beans 2 quarters & an half, & there is an horse that he was bid four pounds for a little while ago. If you like to have these assigned over to you as a security, if you lay down the money, it will be goodness in you, & I believe Mr Conquest Jones will never have anything unless he lays hold of this opportunity. I am in haste

Your humble serv^t
H.P.

For /

Mr Welchman sen^r· attorney
at law at Brackley /
This.

100. H.P. to John Wentworth (Cresswell)

Shalstone,
January the 21st, 1741.

Sir! /

In answer to yours, can acquaint you Goodm^n· Enoch was always esteemed a civil neighbour, but as to his circumstances & management of his farm I know nothing of them. He offered to take a bargain of me, but I refused him by reason he said I sent to him on that account when I did not, neither did my mother think him sufficient for the taking of it. I desire your privacy on what I now write & you shall know more when I see you. We long to wait on you but (t)here have been so many rogues hereabouts that we have not as yet had courage to go abroad, & with our hearty respects to Mrs Wentworth & yourself, I am Sir!

Your very humble servant
H.P.

For /

John Wentworth a͡ls Cresswell
Esqre at Lillingston Lovell
This.

101. H.P. to Mr Land

Shalstone,
Friday, September 19th, 1746.

Sir! /

My tenant Goodman Jeeves died last night of the small pox & is in a
pretty large arrears of rent, & I find myself under a necessity to distrain – I
have never had the small pox myself, so if it is suitable to you, I desire you
will come over yourself with the bearer to make the distress – if you can't
come, pray let me know by the bearer wch will oblige

Your h͠fe serv^t
H.P.

P.S. My mother joins with me in
     our compliments to you.

For /
    Mr Land Attorney at Law at Buckingham
       This.

102. H.P. to Mr Land

Shalstone,
Novemb. 14th, 1746.

Sir! /

Here has been one Coles (who lately rented of Mr Bathurst of Mixbury)
to offer to take a bargain of me & pretends he has the wherewithal to take it.
I hear you were concerned in distraining him for rent, so beg the favour of
you to let me know what you judge his circumstances to be, & if he is capable
of renting a bargain between fifty & sixty pounds a year. – This will be a
favour to

Your humble servant
H.P.

P.S. If it does not suit your leisure to send an answer per bearer, pray favour
     me with it by Shem Baxter's postboy next Tuesday night.

For /
    Mr Land Attorney at Law at Buckingham.

103. H.P. to Mr South

Shalstone,
Wednesday, Novr the 18th, 1747.

Mr South, /

Mr Land the Attorney of Buckingham acquaints me that you want a bargain of about three score pounds a year. I have a bargain of seven yard lands in the open field with the homestall to set next Lady Day. The yearly rent is eight pounds the yard land & there is a close let with them, wch altogether make sixty three pounds a year – if this suits you, I shall be willing to accept you as a tenant. Your answer directed to be left for me at Mr Benam's at the Horseshoe alehouse at Brackley will oblige

Your friend to serve you
H.P.

For /
    Mr South at Astrop
        This.
    Carriage paid two pence.

104. H.P. to John Wentworth (Cresswell)

Shalstone,
Novemb^r the 22th, 1747.

Sir /

James Greaves rents £39 a year of me, most of it ploughed land, & leaves my bargain at Lady Day next. I heard he had a mind to take a grazing bargain, for less stocks than that ploughed land & I believe him sufficient to rent your bargain of £50 a year. He is a very civil fellow & I hope he will make you a good tenant. My mother has been ill and taking mercury some time, otherwise we had waited on you & Mrs Wentworth before this. We are very glad to hear of your healths which we wish may continue, & desire our compliments may be acceptable to you both & I am Sir!

Your obliged humble servant
H.P.

For /
    John Wentworth Esq
        at Lillingston Lovell
            This.

105. H.P. to Alexander Croke

Shalstone,
January the 9th, 1748.

Sir! /

I have lately had several young ash trees cut up in Shalstone Cowpasture
& such shameful destruction made of the wood there that, unless I can put
a stop to it, in a little time I shall have no wood left there. Tho' I give the
poor of Shalstone leave to pick up rotten wood there, tho' there is enough
for 'em they won't be content without making such waste as above, so I
desire you would send me a Lodging Warr^{t.} to search not only for the
present but as often as any offences shall be committed on my wood &c. If
it should require two Justices hands to it, must beg the favour of you to get
another Justice's hand besides your own, wch you may do at the next Qr.
Sessions at Aylesbury if business should call you there, & send it by some
hand or other to Mr Wallbank's at Buckingham. But if you don't attend the
Sessions, pray send the Warrant by the bearer signed by yourself under a
cover, & I will procure another hand to it. Pray don't inform the bearer of
anything of this lest it should take wind. What the Warrant comes to
he has orders to pay. This will much oblige

Your very humble serv^t
H.P.

Pray let the Warr^t be directed not only to the Constable of Shalstone, but
to any other Constable in the County, or otherwise if they should abscond
they will not be so easily taken.

For /

Alexander Croke Esq at
Marsh Gibbon /
This.

106. H.P. to Mr Spiers

Shalstone,
Wednesday, Jan^{ry} the 31st, 1749.

Mr Spiers /

Now my ash is viewed, I desire you will come over here tomorrow or

G

next day at farthest to see it if you should like it. I intend to cry a sale of it & my tenant must have time to brew ale[1] against the sale day, or otherwise I should not be so urgent to see you so soon and am

Your friend to serve you
H.P.

For / Mr Spiers a wheelwright
  to be left at the Black Swan Inn
   at Brackley

107. H.P. to John Elms

Shalstone,
Wednesday, April the 3^{d.}, 1751.

Goodm^{n.} Elms /

Goodman William Hobcraft has cut the thorns off from a lea in Daw's Corner, part of wch lea I suppose belongs to me & part to him, but the exact bounds of it we can't agree about. As your father Elms rented this lea & the land near it, I suppose you must know how far my ground went there, & must entreat of you to let me have a line or two from you, directed to be left for me at Mr Blencow's an ironmonger's at Brackley next Wednesday, what day you can come here on to decide this affair, & I will send word to Wm. Hobcraft to attend then. Must desire you to be here by ten o'clock in the morning because it will take some time in laying this matter out; any day will do but Wednesday or Saturday. I shall be ready to satisfy you for your trouble in coming over. This will oblige

Your humble servant
H.P.

For /
 Goodman John Elms at M^r
  Rose's at Charlton
   This.
 Carriage paid twopence.

---

1 Liberal dispensations were usually thought to expedite these occasions, and to ensure that bidding would be brisk.

108. H.P. to John Elms

May the 25th, 1751.

Goodman Elms,

Goodm^{n.} Wm. Hobcraft was not satisfied with your staking out the lea, he not being there himself, & I have sent to him to fix a day for attending this matter & he has appointed next Friday morning, so must desire you to be here by eleven o'clock on Friday morning next, & I shall be ready to satisfy you for your trouble in coming here, & desire you to let me have a line or two from you (directed for me) to be left at Mr Blencow's an ironmonger's at Brackley next Wednesday, that you will come over here on Friday morning next, which will oblige

Your humble servant

H.P.

For /

Goodman John Elms at
Mr Rose's at Charlton /
This.
Carriage paid 2^{d.}

109. H.P. to William Hobcraft

Shalstone,
April the 28th, 1752.

Goodman Hobcraft /

On Wednesday last, I was at Brackley market where I met Mr John Jones of Wappenham and related to him the little matter of dispute between you & me, & he says he will be sure to be at Brackley on Wednesday next about 12 o'clock. You may hear of him at the Crown inne, & he says he will endeavour to convince you as to this affair. I entreat you will meet them at that time, & am

Your friend to serve you

H.P.

P.S. Let me know what resolution you come to.

For /

Mr William Hobcraft at Finmere.
This.

(c) THE PUREFOYS AND RURAL CRAFTSMEN

110. H.P. to William Gunn

Shalstone,
April 17th, 1736.

I wonder you neglect digging the stone for the time will be elapsed wch you have to do it in, & if you should not be ready it will hinder the carpenters' work, therefore you must be sure not to be behind hand. When you come this way, let me see you wch will oblige

Your friend to serve you
H.P.

To Mr William Gunn
a Mason at Buckingham.

111. H.P. to Mr Jones

Shalstone,
Saturday, April the 24th, 1736.

Mr Jones /
I desire you will send me word by the bearer if you have got any tanner to buy the bark. If you can't get any, I must look out one myself for when I cut the oaks down, the tanner who buys it must set somebody to peal it. Your answer will oblige

Your friend to serve you
H.P.

For /
    Mr Jones a Carpenter
      at Buckingham

112. H.P. to Mr Jones

Shalstone,
May the 29th, 1736.

Mr Jones /
The timber is not brought home as yet, but whenever you will come over to set up the carriage, you may have it brought to the saw pit & enter

on work as soon as you will. Will. Gunn has not dug half his stone & has
stayed away to day. Pray make him come to his work again, for I don't
care how soon 'tis all done & am

Your friend to serve you
H.P.

For / Mr Jones a Carpenter
  at Buckingham /
    This d.

113. H.P. to Oliver Paine

Shalstone,
Wednesday, March the 22nd, 1737.

Mr Paine,

    I imagine young Charles Parker the mason of your town has over
reckoned me for doing the oven at my tenant Mr Hunt's, so we have agreed
to put it to two persons to decide it, and I have chosen you for my referee,
so entreat you will send word by the bearer what day this week you will
come over here on, & Charles Parker's man shall meet you. I believe either
Friday or Saturday will be proper if it suits with your conveniency. I am

Your friend to serve you
H.P.

For / Mr Oliver Paine a
  Baker at Brackley /
    This.

114. H.P. to Charles Parker

Shalstone,
July 2nd, 1738.

Mr Parker /

    You told me you would procure me a load of stone from Brackley pits
that would do Hunt the baker's drain; it must be done now, for he says he
can't bring in his hay till it is done.

When I can have these stones let me know that I may send the team for them, and then you must come yourself & do the drain forthwith. In haste
Yours

H.P.

For /
    Mr. Charles Parker
      jun^{r.} a mason
        at Brackley /
        This.

115. H.P. to Mr Morris

Shalstone,

August the 5th, 1738.

Mr Morris /

As I was on Thursday last at my tenant's Mr Hunt the baker's, I had a complaint about their well which on examination I find to be quite dry.

As you dug the well & engaged to make it good in case it failed of water, I expect you should dig it deeper. If you will come over here tomorrow morning, I shall be at home & then we may talk about it. I am in haste.
Your humble serv^t

H.P.

For / Mr Morris a wells digger
    at Buckingham
      This.

P.S. Don't fail to come. Mr Hunt goes I know not how far for such water as he daily uses in his family.

116. H.P. to Charles Parker

Shalstone,

Saturday, Septemb^{r.} ye 23^d, 1738.

Master Parker /

This is the third day you have been from my work, tho' you promised faithfully you would never leave it till you had finished it – if you don't

come on Monday next, I will set somebody else to work upon it. I think
you are a very unworthy man to neglect it so this fine weather & am
                        Your friend to serve you
                                H.P.

For /
    Mr Charles Parker jun^r.
        a mason at Brackley
            This.
    With speed.

117. H.P. to Charles Parker

                                    Shalstone,
                                    Novemb^r. the 4th, 1738.
Mr Parker /
    I have heavy complaints ab^t the baker's hogsty being not pitched &
Robt Sallmon's chimney not done, so I desire you will not fail to be here on
Monday next at farthest, & bring Master Elms the carpenter along with
you, or if he is engaged in business bring any other carpenter, wch will
oblige
                        Your friend to serve you
                                H.P.

For Mr Charles Parker Junior
    a Mason at Brackley
        This d.

118. H.P. to Philip Leapor

                                    Shalstone,
                                    December 5th, 1738.
Mr Leapor /
    The asparagus beds are dug up & the old roots cleaned out. We have
6 or 8 loads of black rotten muck in our back yard, which may be brought
to the Garden door the day you come on – if it is brought before it may
make a litter, the stableyard is so narrow.
    I desire you will come over the beginning of this next week to trench

the beds & our folks shall be in readiness. Let me know by the bearer what day you will come on, wch will oblige

Yours in haste
H.P.

For / Mr Leapor a Gardiner at
   Brackley /
     This.

119. H.P. to Charles Parker

Shalstone,
August the 20th, 1739.

Mr Parker /

I sent yesterday to Huntmill & the river is exceeding low, & the lime carried down to Mr Friday's barn, so I entreat you will not fail to come & do the wall there tomorrow or next day at farthest – if we lose this opportunity, we may not have another this season. I am

Your friend to serve you
H.P.

For /
   M^r· Charles Parker
     Junr· a mason at Brackley /
       This.

120. H.P. to Zachary Jordan

Shalstone,
June the 3rd, 1740.

Mr Jordan /

The ash trees lie at the sawpit ready to be cut out. You told my mother you would come here before this time to cut them out. Pray don't fail to come some time this week or as soon as you can, wch will oblige

Your friend to serve you
H.P.

For /
   Mr Zachary Jordan a ploughwright
     at Helmdon /
       This.

121. H.P. to James Gibbs

Shalstone,
Decembr the 13th, 1749.

Mr Gibbs /

The bay mare you sold me last, as I was riding her to Brackley market next Wednesday, started with me & threw me in the ford of the river at Westbury Town's end. I fell of[f] her farther side on my head in the river, & received no other damage (thro' God's mercy) but a bruise on the muscle of my right arm which pains me very much. Had not the water saved my fall, it would undoubtedly have been worse with me. After so bad an accident I don't intend to get on her back any more, but must desire you to dispose of her for me. I don't know but you might sell her at next Banbury twelfth fair. The next I have, I resolve, shall be a gelding not above fourteen hands high or there abouts. I have a notion that mares when they go to horse are resty or gamesome, & not fit for me. This mare's cold is quite gone & sound in all respects as far as I know. I should be glad to see you here to take a dinner with me if you'll let me have a line or two from you directed for me to be at Mr Yates senior, a grocer's at Brackley, what day you'll come on. I won't fail to be at home & am

Your humble servant
H.P.

For /
    Mr James Gibbs at Souldern
        This.
    Carriage paid two pence.

4

The Family

IN the landowning class of eighteenth century England, family considerations were almost all intimately bound up in matters relating to the ownership of property. Births, marriages and deaths changed the value and direction of bequests. Dowries, portions and provisions for the unmarried provided business for a specialist branch of the law. It was believed that the estate should support all the members of a family, for whom the nominal owner acted as trustee. To be head of the family therefore involved responsibility for what could be a wide circle of people. A string of unmarried daughters, maiden aunts or unenterprising sons could represent a financial burden of appalling proportions.

The fact that the Purefoys had few close relations in this period was not therefore, without advantages. On his father's side, Henry only had as cousins the Jervoise family of Herriard House in Hampshire, who were descendants of his grandfather's sister. As his natural heirs, Henry took a keen interest in the character and disposition of his likely successors (Letter 130), but otherwise relations were formal rather than warm, and visiting was kept to a minimum. The Jervoises were, however, respectable. The same could not be said for Mrs Purefoy's relations. Her sister, whose death is referred to in the letters, married out of her class and left a son and a daughter in straitened circumstances. This nephew of the Purefoys, Ralph Porter, becomes the anti-hero of many of these letters, in which his mounting criminal activities are recorded with a growing sense of outrage by his aunt and cousin. Relatives of this kind could only be acutely embarrassing. The only remedy lay in publicly advertising a severance of relations, and in following this up with a personal letter putting the matter beyond doubt (Letter 139).

If this were not done, the family would be involved in at least a loss of face, if not in direct financial deprivations.

Family connections were not, however, uniformly irritating. Mrs Porter clearly hoped for preferment in the navy for her son by playing on her relationship with the Purefoys (Letter 126). Mrs Purefoy in turn seems to have relied on her remote cousinage with the Fish family of London for management of her property in the capital. The correspondence with this branch of the family runs continuously through these years, and never appears to be clouded by recriminations or periods of strain. This was the ideal. A family should have been a unit of mutual co-operation and advancement. It was therefore doubly annoying when family renegades like Ralph Porter threatened such a potentially effective system by gratuitously irresponsible behaviour. As Henry Purefoy and his mother pointed out, his delinquency was manifested in spite of repeated offers of assistance. His was a clear breach of a basic code.

There was also another offensive aspect of Porter's behaviour. Surrounded by ancestral portraits and busts, the owners of eighteenth-century estates took a positive pride in 'family'. The fact of continuous ownership for nearly three hundred years was a matter of importance. It was a point of which the county took notice. Not surprisingly therefore, Henry Purefoy was only too anxious to help the antiquarian Browne Willis with his *History of the Hundred of Buckingham* (Letters 137–8). Such a volume, if correctly researched, could only enhance his authority and standing in relation to the other landowning families. Porter's career of fraud and brigandage brought contempt on this record. The abrupt and instinctive imposition of atavistic retribution by Mrs Purefoy would not have been questioned or considered unjust by her contemporaries. The nexus of the family was too precious a thing in the eighteenth century for such attitudes to be tolerated.

122. E.P. to Christopher Farmer

Shalstone,
May the 9th, 1736.

I rece^d Mr Farmer's letter of the 1st instant & am sorry to hear you left York since the Southwark air disagrees with you so much. My son & self wish you better health & shall be very glad to see you at Shalstone when it suits with your conveniency – if you don't know it, Mrs Millicent Clarke, who lived with my father & afterwards with me, lives at the King's Head Tavern over against the church in Islington, which house she keeps & is married again to one Mr Robotham,[1] & my nephew Porter (who lives in Chancery Lane) hath married an heiress out of Lincolnshire of £6,000 fortune as he says. Her maiden name was Cunington & she lived at Lincoln when he married her. Pray if you know anybody of that country, enquire if there be any such place as the manor of Cainby, which he says is devolved to him & his wife's sister by the death of their uncle. This will oblige

Your humble serv^t·
E.P.

P.S. / My son joins with me in our service to you

For / Mr Christopher Farmer

　　at the back of Guy's Hospital

　　　　Southwark.

123. E.P. to Thomas Robotham

Shalstone,
Tuesday, June the 15th, 1736.

. . . We are glad Mrs Robotham is so well as to go to visit Mrs Porter – 'tis well he has got such a good wife & an house well furnished, which I hope he will be contented with. He has wrote a letter here & says we mistrust the truth of what he said. We never said anything about him but to you. Therefore I pray advise him to be at rest for we never did nor shall ever say or do anything to his prejudice. The more he has the better it is for him, for I desire to know no more about it which pray let him know. I have at present a very bad state of health . . ., & am

Your humble serv^t·
E.P.

For /

　　Mr Robotham . . .

　　London.

---

1 See Chapter Five.

124. E.P. to Ralph Porter

Shalstone,
April the 3rd, 1737.

Dear Nephew,

I received your letter, and the small pox has been very much here and all who have had it (but one) died. But at present, 'tis out of our town. When our fears are over shall be glad to see you & Mrs Porter at Shalstone. Jenny mare at present is in great favour, but I have not rode her yet, my leg has been so bad. My son joins with me in love & service to you both, & I am

Your affecte. Aunt
E.P.

For /
    Mr Porter . . .
        London.

125. H.P. to Thomas Robotham

Shalstone,
June ye 14th, 1737.

This requests Mr Robotham as soon as you can after you receive this to go to my cousin Porter & acquaint him that my mother is again much indisposed, and that we can't have any thoughts of his coming to Shalstone till my mother has better health. I would have wrote to him myself but was afraid the letter might by chance miscarry. We are in great hurry, having a farm of an hundred pounds a year fell into our hands, which, joined to this other misfortune, makes it impossible for us to entertain anybody; pray give our love & service to Mr & Mrs Porter. If you have not paid Mr Mulford already, pray pay him as also Mr. Gamull, & let me know the price of 2 tickets in the Bridge Lottery, as also let us have your account that I may know what money to return. My mother & self join in service & respect to you & Mrs Robotham, & I am

Your very humble servt.
H.P.

For /
    Mr Robotham . . .
        London.

126. E.P. to Mrs Porter

Shalstone,
October the 21st, 1739.

Dear Sister /

I received yours a considerable time ago and am glad to hear your son Porter & his spouse were to visit you. We should have been glad if it had been in our power to have done your younger son any acceptable service, but, as it is now war time, I hope you will find it no difficulty to have your expectations answered as to him as he has been bred to sea affairs. All our friends who could have served him are either dead or who have no interest at Court. I have my health pretty well now, all but a sore leg which has been very bad as I have been in health. It is a scorbutic humour & I cannot learn when it is to be well. My son presents his duty to you & we both desire our love & service to your family, & shall be glad to hear of all your healths, which concludes me

Your affect: sister
E.P.

For /
Mrs Porter at
Scarborough
in Yorkshire
By London.

127. E.P. to Thomas Robotham

Shalstone,
March the 8th, 1740.

... I know you used to have acquaintance of Lincolnshire gentlemen, & I desire you would enquire if there be such a person as M^r· Kent an Attorney of Grantham in Lincolnshire, & what character he bears in that country, & what sort of a person of a man he is.

A stranger man came to us as from Mr Porter on the 5th of this instant March at 7 in the morn., & said his name was Kent, and that he was an attorney of Grantham in Lincolnshire. He came as he pretended upon a very impudent errand from Mr Porter, which you shall know more of when I have the character of the man. As to his person, he was very near six foot high, of a fair & fresh complexion, with a white periwig, a short loose greatcoat, & a blue-grey coat with gold buttons, & a black waistcoat, & a coloured handkerchief about his neck, & had a young fellow with him about 20 years old in a black cap. Both of them were very well mounted & they lay the night before they came here at the Lord Cobham's Inn, as he said. When you have enquired if there is such a person & his character, let me know by the post as soon as may be, wch will oblige

Your humble servant
E.P.

P.S. Our service & respects are with yourself & Mrs Robotham.
For / Mr Robotham . . .
London.

128. E.P. to Thomas Robotham

Shalstone,
March the 18th, 1740.

I rece^d Mr. Robotham's letter of the 12th instant. I am glad to hear Mr. Kent is a man of good character, for he came in such a manner I was afraid he was an incendiary, his coming so early in the morning & refusing to send in his business, and desiring to speak with me alone without anybody's letter or name to introduce him very much surprized me, till my son looking out of the window & asking him his business, he said he came from Mr Porter, upon which my son asked him to walk in, & we went down to him. Upon my enquiring his business, he told me he came from Mr Porter, who said that I would be bound with him for £3,000, and that one Mr. Preston was to advance the money & asked if such a person did not live hereabouts. I told him there was no such person as Mr Preston in this country, & that I would not be bound with Mr Porter for 3 farthings, & that I had not seen him these 7 years. Mr Kent seemed shocked when I told him I had not seen Mr Porter for 7 years, & that I would not be bound with him, & so took his leave, & I could not help telling him he came with the Tale of a

Tub without a bottom.¹ To be sure, Mᵣ Porter must tell him some strange story to give him an assurance to come in such a manner. I desire you will write to Mᵣ Porter & let him know that Mᵣ Kent called here on the 5ᵗʰ of March last in this manner, & that unless Mᵣ Porter writes me word by the post that he never had any will of mine in his keeping, & that I never was bound with him nor for him for any sum of money whatsoever, nor ever promised to be bound with him, & that I never gave him any sum of money more than 2 or 3 guineas at a time, and that I have not seen him these 7 years last past, – if Mᵣ Porter does not comply with this, & that soon to, I shall be obliged to advertize something of this nature in the newspapers.

I seldom go into any company in this country, but I am told Mᵣ Porter reports I gave him £4,000 this last year, besides other sums before, wᶜʰ· you know is false. I pray you would not spare Mᵣ Porter, but inform him of all these particulars, for I am really apprehensive he has some mischievous design against me, to prevent wᶜʰ I am advised by my friends to advertize what I have mentioned unless he makes me the above acknowledgement, for I think, if Mᵣ Porter has no ill design in this matter, it is well if he is in his right senses, for I never heard of such a thing in my life before. We both join in our service & respects to yourself & Mʳˢ Robotham, & I am

Your humble servant
E.P.

For /
    Mᵣ Robotham . . .
      London.

129. E.P. to Mʳˢ Jane Conington

Shalstone,
December the 31ˢᵗ, 1740.

Madam /

I receᵈ yours of the 20ᵗʰ instant, & in answer thereto I do assure you I have never given my nephew Ralph Porter one farthing of money since he has been married nor some time before, nor never shall give him anything

---

¹ A satirical novel by Dean Swift. The sense of this expression is that the unfortunate Mr Kent has no case to make.

for I have a son of my own & if I had ten times what I have I would not leave it him. My nephew lost my favour on account of some little indiscretions here, &, soon after, I heard he had bought chambers at Barnard's Inn, or rather built them at a great expence, & put himself in a garb of velvet silk, gold & silk, & a fine diamond ring at a greater expence, & after that I discarded him knowing that his circumstances could not bear anything of that kind, for I suppose my sister Porter has £40 a year in land at Old Newton in Yorkshire for her life & he has it after her in fee, & I suppose my sister may have to the value of £1,000 besides at her disposal, as he told me for I have not seen my sister Porter since the year 1716.

As to what D^r· Trimnell said about my giving my nephew a great sum of money, I heard it from several of my neighbours that Dr Trimnell should say so, & when the D^r· was at Astrop Wells last season, I took care to send him word there was nothing in it. I look on the Doctor to be a very worthy gentleman & am sorry to hear my nephew has used him as he has. I doubt my nephew takes his baseness from the Porters, for I never knew any of my father or mother's kindred behave as he has done. I think his father made a poor improvement of the fortune he had with my sister, for he had £3,000 with her at my father's death besides what he had with her before.

I once thought my nephew Porter as likely to get an estate by his business as any young fellow whatsoever, & if I could have prevailed on him to have been advised by me & my son, we thought no otherwise than to have encouraged him & to have been kind to him.

I hope Mrs Porter as an heiress has kept her land to herself at least. He reported, when he came to Town & bought the chariot & fine equipage, that he had £400 a year in land left him by the Conington family exclusive of you, & there was a report that he had got your money in his hands w^{ch}· came from a merchant in the City, & that he had put £800 thereof in the late Alderman Childs' hands to take up to pay tradesmen, & he once gave out he had my will in his keeping wch is entirely false. I aver this for truth and wish it may be serviceable to you.

I am, Madam,

Your humble servant

E.P.

For /

   Mrs Jane Conington

      . . . in Lincoln in Lincolnshire.

   By London.

H

130. H.P. to Thomas Jervoise

Shalstone,
January the 17th, 1741.

Sir! /

My mother & self designed ourselves the pleasure of waiting on you at Herriard last summer, but were disappointed. My present request is to let me know by the post your second son his Christian name & the Christian names of his four sons as they be in seniority of age. We hope to wait on you at Herriard some time next summer & in the mean time shall be glad to hear you enjoy good health, & with both our respects & good wishes for yourself & family, I am Sir!

Your affect: kinsman
& very humble servant
H.P.

For /
Thomas Jervoise Esq.
at Herriard
near Basingstoke
in Hampshire
By way of London

131. E.P. to Thomas Robotham

Shalstone,
June the 13th, 1741.

... I have never heard from Mr. Porter, but I think he might have mentioned something to you if he had not written to me, but it is like the rest of his proceedings. I can't join with you in sorrow for Mr Porter, but am glad justice has overtook him that there may be some hopes that something may be saved for his wife. I am sorry I have so vile a person so near a kin to me, and shall not trouble my head to advertize him, now his circumstances are such. I am in hopes of seeing a gentleman soon who will give me an account of everything ...

Your hùe serv^{t.}
E.P.

For /
Mr Robotham ...
London.
with a parcel of butter.

132. E.P. to Thomas Robotham

Shalstone,
December the 23rd, 1741.

... Since I wrote to you last, here has been a man who has assumed the name of Fish & pretended to buy the Manor House of Souldern near Bicester in Oxfordshire & other estates of 5 or 6 hundred a year, & to pay for 'em on a day certain, but before the day of payment came he absconded. He has run in debt (as the country says) at Oxford, Banbury, Bicester & Souldern to the sum of 5 or 6 hundred pounds, & on Tuesday the 8th of December about 4 o'clock in the morning, he went towards London with a good deal of plate & money. The country is in pursuit of him, & would be glad to know where he is. The Saturday before he went of[f], a gentleman came to us, who had a writ out against him by the name of Ralph Porter alias Fish, which surprized us very much, & he told us he should be at Brackley on Wednesday following, where he should serve the writ upon him. To convince myself, I sent the footman who lived here when Mr Porter was here & my own present footman to see if he could know him, but he smelt a rat & went of[f] a day before.

Whoever he is, he is a consumate rascal, for he has given a note subscribed R. Fish to one Mr James Gibbs (a grazier & one that we deal with) for £60, who has a wife & severall children, & he has not satisfied the said note.

He went attended with 3 servants on horseback, & one [of] them (to witt) Paul says his master never went out without 3 brace of pistols about him & his 3 servants armed with the like. He has severall times with his men rode thro' Shalstone by our gates & rounded the town fields, & the townspeople took notice of them & brought us word that they thought they were highwaymen. And this Paul the servant says his master gives out that in case my son dies without children, he is heir of Shalstone in spite of anybody, & Paul tells openly such secrets of his master's family that I think it is Ralph Porter.

Pray let me know Mr Porter's agent's name, & find out if you can whether he carries any correspondence with him now. This has put us into the utmost consternation, & Paul & another of the servants lie about the country still as is supposed for no good. All the while you was here last, he was no further of[f] than at the Crown Inn at Brackley at bed & board. We are told that the whole City of London will ring for him, for that his creditors design to advertize him. I could wish poor Mr Gibbs had his money again. When I see you, you shall have more of this at large; with our compliments for the season of the year to you both, am in haste

Your humble serv^t.
E.P.

For /
    Mr Robotham . . .
    London

133. H.P. to Harry Fish

Shalstone,
March the 30th, 1742.

Sir! /

I wrote to you in August last, to desire you to look out for a purchaser for the house in Grub Lane, but have not heard from you since. I had not have given you the trouble of this letter for that only, but I desire to know how many sons you have & the Christian names of them as they be in seniority of age. I suppose you have heard of Mr Ralph Porter's transactions in this country as well as in Lincolnshire & of the £40 reward to apprehend him, & we hear he has mortgaged my estate & got a woman to personate my mother to carry the cheat on more speciously – it has done me no hurt, but the poor gentleman is entirely bit of his money. Your speedy answer will oblige

Your affect: kinsman
& humble servant
H.P.

P.S. We both join in our respects & service
For / Mr Fish . . .
    London.

134. E.P. to Thomas Robotham

Shalstone,
March the 31st, 1742.

. . . My son has received a letter, part of it in the following words:

Sr /   March the 23^d

It is said here that a Lincolnshire gentleman has advertized a reward of forty pounds for apprehending M^r. Porter. This is certainly true & I am persuaded that you have heard it at Shalstone, but whether the following reports have been made known to you or not I am uncertain. It is said that the particular fact of forgery which occasioned the advertizement relates to your estate, that Mr Porter has prevailed upon the advertizer to advance money upon a counterfeit security. It is added that to carry on the cheat better, a well dressed woman passed for Mrs Purefoy & joined with him in the deed. /

I think Mr. Porter is a very wicked man to use his best friends in this manner, for so we should have been to him had he been like ourselves. The postmaster of Greenwich has sent a letter to the postmaster of Brackley to know if one Mr Robinson had any considerable estate at Brackley, for that the said Robinson told him he had, & that he (the postmaster) had trusted him for a horse & eight pounds, & since he read the advertizements of Mr Kent's against Mr Porter, he had great reason to believe it was Ralph Porter, wch. made him give the Brackley postmaster that trouble. If it lies in your way, pray enquire after this & Mr Kent. In the London Evening Post, Mr Porter has advertized to desire the public to suspend all judgment on either side between him & Mr Kent till he publishes his case, & I hope when Mr Porter publishes this case, he will publish his actions in this country. We wish you & Mrs Robotham your healths & with our respects & service am

Your humble servant
E.P.

P.S. Pray don't forget the charger for the blunderbuss & the swan shot.
For /

    Mr Robotham . . .
      London.

135. H.P. to Richard Jervoise

Shalstone,
January 11th, 1743.

Sir! /

I reced both your last łres & in answer to your first, I wondered to hear that the goods at Herriard house went to sale as you say for paymt. of debts, for as I understand by your late father, when Amersden Hall was sold he should clear all his debts, & if I had not reced your letter that you were gone abroad, I should have endeavoured to have seen you when I was in Town.

Since my unhappy kinsman is fallen into yours & Mr Clarke's hands, I question not but you will use him with tenderness & care.

I am at times afflicted with the gout, so can't at present entertain company here, but hope when I come to Town next summer to see you there. My mother & self desire to give you & Mrs Jervoise the compliments of the season, & I am Sir!

Your affect: kinsman &
very humble servant.
H.P.

For /
    Richard Jervoise Esq
       at Mr Huddleston's in
        Bedford Street in
         Covent Garden
          London.

136. E.P. to Susannah Clarke

Shalstone,
February the 16th, 1745.

I received Mrs Clarke's letter of the 4th instant, & am very sorry to hear of my sister's death, as I am that I could not have an account sooner that we might have gone into mourning for her, but now the time is almost expired. I am glad you did not give yourself the trouble of coming to Shalstone, for since I received the barbarous usage from your brother Ralph, I made a resolution never to see or have anything to do with any of the family of the Porters, & thereupon have settled my estate & what I have on my son Purefoy. Ralph was so great a favourite with my son & self, that we used him & intended him as a younger son in the family. His return was that he made me (as far as in him lay) a forgerer & a felon by bringing a woman down to Aylesbury & executing a counterfeit conveyance in my name for £4,946 10s. on Lord Cobham's estate at Westbury, & when the Commissioners set on Ralph's affairs in Lincolnshire, they sent up the deed by the attorney, who saw the woman sign it, to see if I was her, & when he saw me, he acknowledged I was not the woman, but that she was taller & bigger than me. This transcendent villany occasioned me a great deal of trouble as well as charge. Ralph also took an house in our neighbourhood & cheated the country of what plate & goods & money he could, & then made of[f] with it, which was a great trouble & disgrace also to us. The reason I did not acquaint my sister with this was I was not willing to add to her sorrow. I have not heard from her these 4 or 5 years; then she said she had a son at sea & desired us to endeavour to get some preferment in the navy for him, but I acquainted her it was not in my power. 'Tis well if Ralph is dead, otherwise, as he would have put an halter about my neck, I fear 'twould have been his fate. Adieu /

E.P.

For / Mrs Susannah Clarke living
   near Allbrough gates in
     Scarborough
      Yorkshire

137. H.P. to Browne Willis

Shalstone,
March the 2^{d.}, 1745.

Sir! /

    I am favoured with yours of the 27th instant as likewise with another letter before that containing the Eccl'a͡l History of Shalstone, both which are very perfect acco^{ts.} of what they contain. As to the fee in the Herald's Office, I will pay it you when I have the favour of seeing you. I have nothing more to request of you now but to have the civil history of Shalstone from the Conquest down to the present time, wch. I hope I shall have an opportunity to accomplish when I have the pleasure of waiting on you at Shalstone. If I could have the favour of you to dictate to me, I think verily I could take it down in an hour or an hour & an half's time. If I could have the satisfaction of having your company one night, we have a little bedchamber for your man to lie in next to your bedchamber. With thanks for all favours, I am Sir! /

Your obliged h͡le serv^{t.}
H.P.

For /
    Brown Willis Esq at the
      Plough Inn in Carey street near Lincoln's Inn /
        London

138. H.P. to Browne Willis

Shalstone,
Octob^{r.} the 19th, 1745.

Sir! /

I have sent you enclosed the pedigree of my family, &, when you have finished Shalstone affair, I beg you'll let me have a copy of it. If your amanuensis, or any writing master or such sort of a person, would transcribe it for me from your manuscript as to what relates to Shalstone – I would satisfy them for so doing. My mother joins with me in our humble services, & I am Sir!

Your very humble servant
H.P.

For /

Browne Willis Esq. at his seat
at Whaddon Hall.

139. E.P. to Mrs Susannah Clarke

Shalstone,
July the 16th, 1747.

I received Mrs Clarke's letter & am sorry for your loss if it be so. 'Tis well you have something left to maintain you; if your mother would have been ruled by me, you would have had her fortune when my father died which was £3,000, but nothing would satisfy her but to cancel her marriage settlement.

God bless my eyesight, I desire never to see any of the Porter's family any more. Direct what estate you have anywhere, for I desire none of it.

Adieu.
E.P.

For / Mrs Susannah Clarke . . .
    Yorkshire /
By way of London.

5

The Purefoys and London

ALTHOUGH London lay less than sixty miles from Shalstone, it was for the Purefoys a very distant place. As the London Season grew more and more elaborate in the early eighteenth century, considerable expertise and considerable wealth were required to negotiate its traps and pitfalls with success. Countrymen therefore viewed the capital with suspicion. In his eyes the Londoner was almost always a cheat, was always ready to laugh or sneer at a provincial accent, and was always anxious to take advantage of innocence or naïvety. The antipathy between the capital and the counties provides one of the standard comic mechanisms of the Restoration and Augustan periods, and had a sharp political impact. For people like the Purefoys, London was to be emulated and feared at the same time. The intentions of anything or anyone connected with the capital could never be considered honourable.

Consequently, the Buckinghamshire gentry dealt with London by indirect means. For the simple communication of goods to be bought, sold or repaired, they relied heavily on the services of carriers. The account books make it clear that the total cost of this service rarely exceeded two or three pounds a year. It was, however, an undertaking full of risk. When their first carrier, Webster, went bankrupt in 1738, the Purefoys took care to tie his successor to a firm contractual agreement. Mrs Purefoy noted accordingly that 'my Son Purefoy agreed with the said Mr Eagles to carry for 2^s 6^d the hundred weight for All that is a quarter of an hundred weight, All under to be accounted Parcells. Wee to carry our Things to Buckingham to Him, and to fetch Them Home from Thence.' The county carrier, calling at an agreed London inn twice a week, was the usual channel of communication in an age when travelling was far from easy or comfortable. It was certainly the agency preferred by the Purefoys.

For more important purposes than the dispatch of a parcel or letter, it was usual for county families to appoint a London innkeeper as their agent in the capital. Innkeepers were an obvious choice for this position, in that their trade brought them into contact with all sections of London society and its gossip. Equally, an inn was the obvious *entrepôt* between a London tradesman and his provincial customers. As a result the innkeeper was a considerable leader of opinion at the lower levels of eighteenth century society. Most of the letters in this section are addressed to a member of this fraternity. Thomas Robotham, proprietor of the King's Head in Islington, had married one of Mrs Purefoy's former maids, and was therefore personally known to the family. The King's Head is mentioned by Pepys in his diary, and seems to have been one of the more considerable houses in North London. He shared the Purefoy commission with a certain Peter Moulson of Cursitor's Street, a wine merchant of some importance and a member of the Vintner's Company. Both seem to have performed their tasks without being paid, although they would clearly have the temporary use of sums which the Purefoys placed in their hands from time to time.

As the letters suggest, the range of tasks performed by these two men was great. They were intermediaries between the Purefoys and London trades-men. They were financial advisers on the question of stocks and shares. They interpreted the trends in London fashion (Letter 143). They paid the Land Tax on behalf of their patrons (Letter 142). These two men in fact guided their provincial employers through the tortuous customs and practices of the capital. In return, the Purefoys responded with an assiduous and conscientious hospitality (Letter 144), and expressed themselves ready to help either of these families in the event of some unforeseen disaster (Letter 150). As Fielding's Squire Western discovered, London, without the assistance of such men, could be unbelievably perplexing and sinister. The first section of this chapter demonstrates just how useful such men could be.

An agent of this kind was particularly necessary if a county family was trying to cope with the management of property in London. As the second half of this chapter indicates, endless time could be lost in discussions about broken locks, unpainted walls or smoking chimneys if there were not a trusted representative on hand to deal immediately with problems of this kind. Even so, the trouble which the Purefoys ran into with their two putative tenants, Meredith and Barnard, was sufficiently irritating. In 1738 alone, they were forced to spend £42 17s. ½d. on repairs, in order to secure a firm contract with their tenant. Given postal delays and the difficulty of bringing any direct pressure to bear over a distance of sixty miles, negotiations with a recalcitrant tenant could be infinitely wearing. A totally industrious and reliable London agent was the only way of circumnavigating the problem. The Purefoys themselves visited London only infrequently, regarding as excessive the expenditure and discomfort involved in such expeditions.

The evidence provided by this chapter allows a direct and satisfying account of the relationship between one provincial family and the capital. The Purefoys were involved with London to a certain extent. They bought its stocks and shares (Letter 171), and they envied its fashions. But equally, London gave them a great deal of trouble, and could not be easily handled. Agents or intermediaries had to be trusted far more than the Purefoys would have been willing to trust any local tradesman or entrepreneur. London was a dark, miraculous and awesome entity, which was best kept at arm's length. The Purefoys preferred to do business and find pleasure nearer home.

(a) LONDON AGENTS

140. E.P. to Thomas Robotham

Shalstone,
Wednesday, July the 14th, 1736.

I reced. Mr Robotham's letter of the 8th instant, and my son has his repeating watch safe again. It goes true at present. Pray pay Mr Belchier four pounds & take a receipt in full of all demands from him. I have better health than I had but my leg will not be well. I am afraid my fever fell down in it. We shall be glad to see Mrs Robotham at Shalstone when it suits with her conveniency, & I thank you for doing my errand to Mr Porter. My son has returned you five pound this next week by Mr Webster[1] who comes into

---

1 The first of a succession of Buckinghamshire carriers to be employed by the Purefoys. He was declared bankrupt in 1738. Since others of his profession seem to have suffered similarly, it would seem that the carrier trade was not the most secure form of employment.

Town on Tuesday next about noon, & my son desires you will subscribe four pounds for four lottery tickets[1] for him, & he will return you the money for the other subscription in due time.

This long vacation, I desire you will enquire me out the lowest price of a second hand chair for 2 men to carry me to church in. Pray get me 4 dozen yards of lace the same to the pattern; if you can't have it ready made, there is a man keeps a little lace shop over against St. Clements Church on the side next the Thames. He will make it at two & twenty pence or two shillings the dozen yards. I desire you will buy me the last book that came out about the Scarborough Spa Waters. I think it was wrote by one Dr. Shaw. We both join in our service & respect to yourself & Mrs Robotham, & I am

Your humble serv^{t.}
E.P.

For /
    Mr Robotham . . .
        London

141. H.P. to Peter Moulson

Shalstone,
August the 10th, 1736.

Sir! /

I am favoured with yours of the 3rd. instant. As to Mr Price the Clergyman's daughters, we will let them alone. My mother has a God daughter who was partly bred up under her care. I may fairly say she is a girl of as sharp sense as any in England & as striving & housewifely as may be, & can sow well & understands to do everything in an house – if she had no fortune, if she was to be sold, she is worth five hundred pounds. As to her person it is agreeable enough, & her fortune is £200 down & £200 at the death of her mother, who is upwards of 60 years of age. This nobody can hinder her of & she has a chance to have more. Whether this takes or no, we shall be glad to see you here in your return from Wiltshire, & wishing

---

[1] The state-sponsored lottery was becoming a major source of government revenue in the eighteenth century. Between 1694 and 1784, forty-two such lotteries were set up (see T. S. Ashton, *An Economic History of England in the Eighteenth Century*, London: 1955, pp. 24–25).

you a good journey we both join in service & respect to you, & I am with real esteem

Your very humble serv^{t.}
H.P.

For /

    Mr Moulson . . .

      London.

142. H.P. to Peter Moulson

Shalstone,
January the 29th, 1737.

Sir ! /

I am favoured with yours of the 15th of last month together with your account – My mother has this week ordered you £10 / by Webster, wch. with your 2 quarters rent overbalances this account when you pay the Land Tax & the Ground Rent. Pray let me know – The wine and everything we have of Mr Moulson is always good, wch. we shall be proud to acknowledge . . .

Your humble serv^{t.}
H.P.

For /

    Mr Peter Moulson . . .

      London.

143. E.P. to Thomas Robotham

Shalstone,
July the 24th, 1737.

I received Mr Robotham's letter of the 1st instant, wch. I had answered before now, but my son has been very much out of order but I thank God he is now something better. Be sure buy the lottery tickets before they begin drawing, but for the time of buying them between this & then my son leaves it to you – I desire Mrs Robotham will send me a pattern of the newest fashioned dressed night clothes & rufles and a pattern of the newest fashioned mobb. We both join in service & respect to you & Mrs Robotham, & I am

Your humble serv^t.
E.P.

For /
  Mr Robotham . . .
    London.

144. H.P. to Peter Moulson

Shalstone,
Septemb^r. the 17th, 1738.

Sir! /

I hope you & Mr Price got well to Town, tho' your horses went from our house without any corn, wch. is a concern to my mother & self. For the future, I hope you will take the liberty as I do whatever I go (that is) to command what meat you judge proper for your horses & to order your servant to call for it. It is such a thing as never happened with us before, & I am really ashamed of it. I have had the good fortune to catch a brace of young hares & desire your acceptance of them with a shoulder of venison, being of the last buck wch. was killed in the forest this season, or otherwise it might have been a better piece. They are sent this day (carriage paid) by the Buckingham carrier . . .

We both join in our service & respect to you & Miss Moulson, not forgetting Mr Price & I am, Sir!

Your very humble serv^t.
H.P.

For /
  Mr Moulson . . .
    London.

145. H.P. to Peter Moulson

Shalstone,
December the 24th, 1738.

Sir! /

I was yesterday at Buckingham, & find Webster the carrier is about to break, and I find it is not safe for you to send the wine by him, therefore desire you to defer sending the wine till further orders. I hope to get me a new carrier quickly, & then you shall hear from me. My mother's & my service waits on you & Miss Moulson, wishing you both a merry X^tmas and a happy new year, & I am with real esteem

Your very humble serv^{t.}
H.P.

For /

    Mr Moulson . . .
      London.

146. H.P. to Peter Moulson

Shalstone,
January the 18th, 1743.

Sir! /

I have received the runlet of wine & the account, & my mother will order you payment soon. We heartily congratulate you & your daughter on her marriage & wish the young couple all the felicity this world can afford & our best service waits on them. We shall be sure to make use of Mr Vaughan when we want anything in his way. My mother little thought he was to be the happy man tho' she used the shop many years.

The reason I write to you before I send an order for the money is that I have a friend who has two livings fell to him, & he wants to be a nobleman's chaplain to qualify him to hold them both. As you are intimate with my Lord Shaftesbury's Steward & other nobleman who may deal with you for wine, I do imagine now the Parliament sits, you might have interest enough to procure a Scarf[1] for him on paying what is usual in that case. If the English peers should chance to be full a Scotch peer will do. This will be a favour both to me and the gentleman, if in your power. The benefice being vacant, I entreat you would let me know in a week's time whether you are like to succeed in this affair.

We both join in our best services & respects to you & I am Sir!

Your very humble serv^{t.}
H.P.

For /

    Mr Moulson . . .
      London.

---

1 By a law of Henry VIII, the number of chaplains a nobleman might have was regulated. Each chaplain was, however, allowed to apply for a dispensation to be permitted to hold two benefices at once.

147. H.P. to Mr Mulford

Shalstone,
August the 11th, 1743.

Sir! /

I understand by Mr Land, the attorney of Buckingham, that you set your first floor. An acquaintance of mine whose character is unexceptionable will want a first floor and a bed chamber, 2 pair of stairs backwards, with a garret for servants. I could not tell how to recommend a more honest family than your own. Pray let me know by the Saturday's post if you can accommodate me in this affair, & if your house is clear of the smallpox, wch will oblige

Your humble serv^{t.}
H.P.

P.S. / My mother joins with me in our compliments to yourself & Mrs Mulford.

For / Mr Mulford in Cursitor's Street in Chancery Lane London.

148. E.P. to Mr Mulford

Shalstone,
Novemb^{r.} the 16th, 1743.

I rece^d Mr Mulford's letter of the 22nd of October last, which I had answered before now but that the table clock stood still & would not go, & I was forced to send to the man who manages our clocks – He set it on going & it went 3 days, & I thought he did nothing but wind it up & strike it, and when it stood still again I did the same, & it has went ever since which has been above a week – I asked him what might be the matter with it, and he said that he believed it was the newness of the work that made the wheels stop – I asked him to take it to pieces. He said no, he did not care to meddle with another mans work & that he hoped it would go without – We did not forget to jog it as you bid us, but that would not do.

If you will send the vouchers for the Land Tax, I will order you payment, & desire you will give us what information you can in case it should stop again, for if it does not go true it will be of no use to us & we shall not tell

what to do with it. My sons & my service & respects attend yourself &
Mrs Mulford & the young gentleman & I am Sir! /

Your humble servant
E.P.

For /

    Mr Mulford in Cursitors Street
      in Chancery Lane /
      London

149. H.P. to George Vaughan

Shalstone,
April the 4th, 1744.

Sir! /

    I desire you will send me 5 yards of silver lace to bind a waistcoat as good
& fashionable as any is worn – as also two dozen & four silver twist buttons
for the waistcoat, and enough of fashionable silver lace to lace four pair of
shoes for my mother, & a yard of narrow silver lace to go up the seam behind
the shoes. Send these by the Buckingham carrier . . . Send your bill with them
& will order you payment, & with our compliments to yourself & M^rs
Vaughan, am Sir!

Your humble servant
H.P.

For /

    Mr George Vaughan at the
      Golden Ball near Arundel Street
      in the Strand.
      London.

150. E.P. to Mrs Read

Shalstone,
June the 11th, 1746.

I hope Mrs Read will excuse this trouble, & satisfy me in the following
particulars if it is in your power. I have heard that on Mrs Robotham's
marrying Mr Robotham, that she had by articles of agreement one hundred
pounds to dispose of as she should think fit at her death, & that she designed
it for her neice Nelly. We hear Mr Robotham is going to be married – if so
I suppose Nelly will go from him – I would not write to Mr Robotham

I

nor to Nelly about this affair for fear of making a difference between them, for I think he cannot go on without her in case he does not marry for Mrs Robotham's sake. I wish Nelly very well and should be glad to advise her in any respect, and I dare say you will do the same – & let me know how Nelly goes on with him or if she goes from him. This will much oblige

Your humble servant
E.P.

P.S. / I desire you will not let Nelly nor Mr Robotham know anything of
    this; pray my son's & my service to your husband.
For / Mrs Read a Baker near the Church in
    Islington near London.

151. E.P. to Mrs Russell

Shalstone,
April the 26th, 1747.

I received Mrs Russell's ĺre of the 23^d instant, & am sorry to hear Mr Robotham died in such bad circumstances. It will be right in you to remove your clothes & anything else that is yours out of the house immediately, for if the landlord for rent or for any execution should come on the premises, they will take what they find thereon to satisfy their debt. There is nobody shall wrong you if I can help it. Mr Robotham told me he gave you all your aunt's linen and clothes, wch. will be necessary for you to secure, & I shall be glad to know if there is any writing drawn to settle the hundred pounds on you, for Ralph Porter told me Mr Robotham sealed such a writing, & if you can find any such thing, I will endeavour to see you have justice done you, if there is anything left after payment of debts. For the butter account, it stands thus:—

	£	s.	d.
From the 13th Septr. 1746 to the 1st of Novr following, being 8 weeks butter at 2^{s.} 6^{d.} a week	1	0	0
From 8th Novr. 1746 to 21st March following, being 20 weeks butter at 3^{s.} a week, all but one week when there was but 4 pounds sent	2	19	0
From 28th March 1747 to 25th April following, 5 weeks butter at 2^s 6^d a week		12	6
	£4	11	6

On the 11th of September 1746, Mr Robotham reckoned here at Shalstone with me & my son, & gave us a receipt in full & we gave him one, so we desire to know what he has laid out for us since that time. I don't know anything he could pay for us unless it be Mr Potts the newsman and for the oysters. My son joins with me in our service to you, & should be glad to hear how you go on, & wish you may find it better than you expect. I suppose some of the creditors will administer, but you must not meddle with anything but what is your own. I shan't send any more butter, wch. concludes me

Your friend to serve you

E.P.

P.S. Pray let me know if your uncle was buried where your aunt is.

For / Mrs Russell . . .
London.

152. H.P. to Mr Moulson

Shalstone,
March the 24th, 1749.

Sir! /

I chanced to catch an hare, wch. I desire your acceptance of (carriage paid). We have great talk here that the earthquake is to return that day month it was before in a very terrible manner.[1] We shall be glad to see you & M^r & Mrs Vaughan & George the Second here, where you will all meet with an healthy welcome as tho' you were at home, for I don't know but your kind invitation to your house saved both my mother's & my life, the small pox then being so much in Town. We shall be glad to hear how you have disposed of our stocks & pray pay your good neighbour, Mr Turner

---

[1] It was a common belief in the early eighteenth century that earthquakes and other natural phenomena ran in fixed cycles. On the anniversaries of mild earth tremors, London would be evacuated by all who could afford to move away. Such occurrences also invited metaphysical speculations on the approaching end of the world, or on possible Divine comments about the corrupt state of English politics.

the sadler, six shillings & six pence for a bridle & take rec^t. in full from him. My mother joins with me in our compliments, & I am Sir!

Your obliged humble serv^t.
H.P.

For /
  Mr Moulson in Wood Street
    in Cheapside
      London
With an hare carriage paid.
P.S. I thank God we have had no earthquake here.

(b) LONDON PROPERTY

153. H.P. to Peter Moulson

Shalstone,
Sunday, 29th February, 1735.

Sir! /

...The house is leased to my mother for 40 years from Michaelmas 1710 – and if the tenant whom you recommend is willing to take it for the residue of the term, my mother is willing to set it at the rent you pay. She has lately been very ill of a cold, but thank God is now somewhat better. We both join in our h^te service to you & I am with much real esteem, Sir!

Your very humble serv^t
H.P.

To Mr Moulson in
  Cursitors Street in
    Chancery Lane
      London.

154. H.P. to Peter Moulson

Shalstone,
Thursday, 29th April, 1736.

Sir! /

My mother rece^d a l^re from Mr Meredith wherein he consents to take the house for 7 years from next Mich^as in case she will new paint it & whitewash it from top to bottom & repair it – You know by your lease you are to keep it in repair & so leave it at the expiration of your term.

She has sent him word she hopes the house does not want painting nor white washing so soon, for that it has never been done yet above once in 9 or 12 years – She consents to paint any particular rooms or part of the house that shall want painting, but, since you want it before your time, thinks you ought [to] contribute 2 parts in 7 towards it. He also mentions you expect that he should pay for the sash window. I hope you will make no words about that, for by that you have taken it out & fitted it up as it was before, it will not be worth your while.

Your very hẗe serv^t

H.P.

P.S. /

We both join in
our service & respect
to you

155. E.P. to Hugh Meredith

Shalstone,

Thursday, 29th April, 1736.

Sir! /

I rece^{d.} yours of the 22nd instant. I hope Mr. Moulson won't insist on taking out the sash window if you like to have it in, for by that he has taken it out & put the bricks in the place & fitted it up again as it was before, he will get no great matter by it, which I will acquaint him of. The marble mantel piece is his. The house was painted when Mr. Moulson came into it, & I have never painted it or whitewashed it but once in 9 or 12 years, so I hope it will do for a lease of 7 years (from next Michãs) as it is.

I am willing to condescend to anything that is reasonable & if there be any particular rooms want painting, I shall be willing to have them new done. When I was in the house last summer, I thought all the upper rooms looked very clean & I hope there are no repairs wanting for Mr Moulson cov^{ts.} in his lease to leave it in sufficient tenantable repair.

I am Sir

Your humble serv^{t.}

E.P.

For /

Mr Hugh Meredith
Attorney at Law at
his Chambers in Lincoln's
Inn / London /

156. E.P. to Hugh Meredith

Shalstone,
May the 19th, 1736.

Sir /

I cannot discommend you for desiring the house to be new painted &
white-washed when you come into it. I admit Mr Moulson can't come into
so just a proposal as to contribute 2 parts in 7 towards the painting, w^{ch.}
will not amount to above fifty shillings especially considering that it is for
his interest & convenience only that it is to be done; it will make a great
hole in my rent if I should paint that house every 4 or 5 years – it is what I
have not been used to for it has been painted but once since the year 1714
only, when it was lately painted for him.

I have wrote Mr Moulson a łre, if he will be 2 parts in 7 for the painting,
I will be at all the charge of the white-washing & set on a painter immediately.
I am sure you can't but think this right. If he had no time in it, I should not
ask him to be at any expense in the painting. He still insists there are no
repairs wanting, so if you should go on to take & he to comply, you must
let me know what particulars are wanting that I may acquaint him of it,
& then I will let you know what things are fixed to the house; 'tis strange
Mr Moulson should expect I should pay for the sash window, for when it
was put in I refused to pay for it & told him I never would . . .

I am a person that don't desire to put upon anybody neither shall any
one put upon me.

There has always hitherto been a good correspondence between M^r
Moulson & me, & if 'tis otherwise now 'tis his fault. I am Sir /

Your humble serv^t
E.P.

For /

Mr Hugh Meredith . . .

P.S. Sir, you were mentioning the Chimneys smoked. I lived in the house
    myself 3 winters & never knew one of them to smoke.

157. E.P. to Hugh Meredith

Shalstone,
May the 25th, 1736.

Sir ! /

In answer to yours of the 22nd instant, I wonder Mr Moulson should be
so much against his own interest as not to comply sooner wth. paying

£2 10s. towards the painting. As to the time when the painting is to be
begun you & he must determine. I did not mention any time you was to
enter, only that the lease was to commence from Mic͠has next because it has
always been set from that time. I hope Mr Moulson does not think me so
silly as to loose a quarter's rent, and as for your hardship in paying the rent
you two must agree upon that.

As to this mantelpiece, he need not have been so violent about it, for
I have bid him what is usual, & I do by him as my son has been done by for
he furnished his Apartm^t· in the new building in Oriel Cot͠t, Oxford with
wainscot hangings & all other goods, & enjoyed them only the 2 last years
he was there, and, notwithstanding nothing was the worse, his successor
paid him but 2 thirds, & by enquiring I find 'tis a common rule in such an
occasion in other places. I do assure Mr Moulson that had I a mantelpiece
six times better than that, before I would knock it to pieces I would give it
to him. I wonder he should be so inveterate for I am sure I have done nothing
but what has been right and handsome by Mr Moulson; if you agree with
him to take the house, it will be a very good way for you to draw the lease
out of hand for 7 years from next Mic͠has & let me have a draft of it, that it
may be executed by you & me & Mr Moulson before the painter is set on,
& then there can be no mistake. I will cov^t· to paint & white-wash. My son's
humble service is with you & I am

Your humble serv^t
E.P.

For /

    Mr Hugh Meredith at his Chambers
       in Lincoln's Inn. London /

158. H.P. to Peter Moulson

Shalstone,
Wednesday, July the 14th, 1736.

Sir! /

I am favoured with yours of the 6th instant, & rece͠d the chocolate w^ch·
my mother thanks you for changing.

If Mr Meredith did agree with you, 'tis a wonder he did not stand to it.
He sent to my mother to know if she would have the mantelpiece – she
sent him word she would give the two thirds for it. However, if it cost you

five pounds she will allow four pounds for it, wch. is more than the two thirds, & will pay you for it in case it is not broke or injured. If the knocker of the street door is gone, you must put up another. As to the lock on the closet door of the back parlour, it was a valuable lock & I hope you will have it mended again – I hope there will be no dispute between anybody for my mother has satisfied Mr Meredith that she will do nothing to the house but paint it, neither will she do that till the lease is executed. She expected the draft of it before now, but will write to Mr Meredith again about it this post – if you can't get the lock mended, you must put on such a lock in its stead as Mr Meredith will like. I believe that to be right. We both join in our service & respect to you, & I am Sir!

Your very ĥle serv^t.
H.P.

For / Mr Moulson in
    Cursitor's Street in
        Chancery Lane /
            London
The last mountain wine you sent is very much liked.

159. H.P. to Peter Moulson

Shalstone,
July the 27th, 1736.

Sir! /

I received yours of the 22^d. instant, & what Mr Meredith means by such unusual delays & being on & off as you mention I cannot account for – The last letter my mother had from him was as follows –

Mad^m.

I have at last agreed with Mr Moulson to enter at Micĥas & become your ten^t. in his stead for the remaining part of his term, to which you are pleased to add 5 more years, & I will if you please send you the draft of a lease for your approbation, who am Mad^m. etc.

He also said there must be a mantelpiece in the dining room, & that was the reason my mother would purchase it or otherwise she has no occasion for a mantelpiece till your term is expired. As for the tiles, she paid for some & has the receipt for how many dozen, but if Mr Meredith does not stand word those things must be all let alone. She has done all she can between you &

has wrote him word twice to send the draft of the lease, but has had no answer.

But if I was in your place, I would call on him myself about it for, if the house stands empty the residue of your term, 'twill be a loss to you & a damage to the house. My mother has done everything you desired, & if Mr Meredith fails 'tis none of her fault – She joins with me in our service & respect, & I am, Sir! /

Your very humble serv^{t.}
H.P.

For /
   Mr Moulson . . .
     London.

160. E.P. to Mr Belchier

Shalstone,
Tuesday, 24th August, 1736.

Mr Belchier /

Mr Hugh Meredith of Lincoln's Inn has wrote me a ĩre dated the 13th instant, and says he is just on going to Wales, and desires me to have the house painted & set in necessary repair by Michaelmas next & the key given to you, & that he will settle all matters with me when he returns – I know not what he means by that, for Mr Moulson is to put it in necessary repair, & I am willing to paint it in case Mr Meredith executes a lease, as he sent me word in July last he would send me a draft of one for my approbation, but he never has. Unless the lease is first executed, I will not paint the house which pray let him know, for I can't tell how to direct a letter to Wales to him. Everything was agreed on & Mr Moulson was to pay fifty shillings towards the painting – I wrote him word I would not set the painter on till the lease was executed, & you see he has took no notice of it. With my son & my service to self & Mrs Belchier, I am

Your humble serv^{t.}
E.P.

For /
   Mr Belchier a cabinet-maker at the
     Sun on the south side of St Pauls Church
       in St Paul's Churchyard.
        London.

161. E.P. to Mr Belchier

Shalstone,
August the 1st, 1738.

Sir! /

I did imagine Mr Meredith had agreed to rent my house in Cursitor's Alley for 5 years longer than Mr Moulson's time – being I never heard from Mr Meredith, I desired Mr Moulson to enquire of him if he designed to stay for the time he bargained for, & Mr Moulson sends me word he told him he was treating ab^{t.} another house & designed to leave mine at Michael-mas.

'Tis true I was to paint the house against his coming in, but then Mr Meredith was to have executed his part of the lease first which he did not, and, if I had painted it, it might have been but for those 2 years & then it would have been for me to have painted for another tenant. Pray let Mr Meredith know that, if he is inclined to take a lease of the house for 7 years or longer, I will now paint the house or do anything that is necessary to be done. Mr Moulson told me Mr Meredith consented I might put up a bill over the door, so I wrote to an acquaintance in town to do so. If Mr Meredith don't stay, if you know of a sufficient tenant, let me know & you will oblige /

Your humble serv^t
E.P.

P.S. I would have wrote to Mr Meredith,
    but I sent 2 or 3 ĺres to him ab^{t.}
    the lease but he never answered them.
    Pray our service to Mrs Belchier.
For / Mr Belchier . . .
    London.

162. E.P. to Thomas Robotham

Shalstone,
May 25th, 1740.

. . . I sent an order to receive my rent of Mr Barnard. He has called often on him, but Mr Barnard's answer is that he is busy in law affairs & that he has a bill for sewers which must be allowed him. I don't know what he means by it. I never paid anything for sewers in my life, it being as I suppose a tenant's tax. Pray call on Mr Barnard when you go to town & know his meaning, & desire him not to make Mr Moulson come after him so, and when you have been with Mr Barnard let me have advice thereof, & what the pitching of the street before his door comes to, & let the 10s 6d be allowed for the lease . . .

Your humble servant
E.P.

For / M^r· Robotham . . .
London.

163. H.P. to H. Fish

Shalstone,
May the 29th, 1740.

Sir! /

My mother received yours of the 22nd instant, and we are sorry to hear of our kinsman Mr John Fish's death; she says she hopes he departed this life without any disgrace to the family & would be glad to know where he is buried. There is a little house & closes in Grub Lane that I believe falls between my mother & you. As I suppose, she would purchase your share of it (if you are willing to part w^th· it) because it was her grandmothers. I desire you will let me know the tenant's name who rents it, & the present yearly rent thereof & in what condition the house & closes & mounds thereof are in. My mother joins with me in our respects to yourself & Mrs Fish and family, & I am

Your affect: kinsman
and humble servant
H.P.

For /
    Mr Fish in Chancery Lane
      near Lincoln's Inn /
        London.

164. H.P. to H. Fish

Shalstone,
August the 2ᵈ·, 1741.

Sir! /

I reced yours of the 7ᵗʰ of last month, & indeed I had a design to have purchased your moiety of the Grub Lane house myself to have made me a freeholder in Hertfordshire,[1] but upon further consideration I think it lies too wide for me to look after & may be troublesome to me.

Since you don't seem inclined to purchase my mother's moiety, she desires you will get a purchaser for it out of hand, which when you have done pray let us hear from you – We both join in service & respect to you all & I am

Your affect: kinsman and
humble servant.

For /

H.P.

Mʳ Fish at the Golden Periwig
in Chancery Lane near Lincoln's Inn. London.

165. E.P. to Thomas Robotham

Shalstone,
Febry. the 16ᵗʰ, 1744.

Sir! /

I received Mʳ Robotham's letter of the 29ᵗʰ of last month . . . I thank you for enquiring for a purchaser for the house in Grub Lane. I admire Mʳ Fish should think of no more than an hundred pound for it.[2] However, I will get my lawyer to look for a chap[3] for it when he comes to town – and I desire you will enquire what you can about it. Pray call on Mʳ Mulford in Cursitor's Alley & ask him if he had my son's letter about the alarum – As to Mʳ Barnard, he need not undervalue the house, for I have one or two that are about it . . .

I am your humble servant
E.P.

For /

Mʳ Robotham . . .
London.

---

[1] A freehold in Hertfordshire would also have given Henry Purefoy a vote in elections for that county. The house in question was in Hatfield.
[2] The house was finally sold for £110 in 1745.
[3] 'Chap' – customer or buyer.

166. E.P. to Thomas Robotham

Shalstone,
February the 24th, 1744.

Sir! /

In my last to M[r] Robotham, I entreated him to call on M[r] Mulford.
I have since received a letter from him – When we were in Town last, he
desired to be a purchaser for the remaining part of the lease of my house in
Cursitor's Alley[1], but now he tells me he has no occasion for it – I believe
the present tenant & he are well agreed together, so I desire you will enquire
either for a purchaser for the residue of the term I have in the house, w[ch] is
five years to come from next Michaelmas, or else for a tenant that he will
take it for such term without any great matter of repairs. We desire yours
& M[rs] Robotham's acceptance of an hare, and with my son's & my respects
& service to you both, I am

Your humble serv[t.]
E.P.

For /

M[r] Robotham . . .
London.

167. E.P. to Peter Moulson

Shalstone,
March the 9th, 1745.

Sir! /

I rece[d] yours of the 21st of January together with my box, & return you
thanks for your care thereof. The red wine is drawn of[f] & meets with
great approbation. I desire you will always let me have such as this. The
stocks & times are so precarious[2] I am afraid to venture at present, so am
seeking out a security in the country. So soon as I can get returns, I will have
my money down in the country. I desire you will send me half an hogshead

---

1 Thomas Barnard took over the rest of the lease on the Cursitor's Alley house for £100
in November 1745, after a great deal of further haggling, when the negotiations with
Mulford finally broke down.
2 One of the few references in the whole Purefoy collection to contemporary national
politics, which were quite clearly a peripheral consideration for most of Henry Purefoy's life. This allusion to the invasion of England by Prince Charles Edward, the
Jacobite Young Pretender, was therefore prompted by considerable anxiety.

of your best old mountain wine by Mr Jones the carrier . . . Pray let me have a l're by the post & your account therein. With thanks for all favours, I am

Your humble servant

E.P.

P.S. My son joins with me in our service & respects

For /

    Mr Moulson in
      London.

168. H.P. to Peter Moulson

Shalstone,
Octob^r· the 5th, 1746.

Sir! /

    I am favoured with yours of the 23^d· of last month, & we give you & M^r & Mrs Vaughan joy of your grandson, & should have been proud to have waited on you at Shalstone . . . I entreat you to favour me with a letter by the post when you send the wine that it may not lie at the carrier's warehouse without our knowing of it. My mother wants a security in the Funds for £400. She can meet with none here for 'tis what she secured to assist us in case the rebels had come forwards, & begs to know what stock at this time she may lay it out in. Both our respects & service wait on you, & I am, Sir!

Your most humble servant

H.P.

For /

    Mr Moulson   } Your bill & will order payment.
      in London   }

169. E.P. to Peter Moulson

Shalstone,
Decemb^r· 10th, 1746.

Sir! /

    I received yours of the 4th instant with the receipt for the 4 per cent Bank Annuities, and I do acknowledge that you have laid out three hundred & ninety six pounds ten shillings (I remitted to you) in these Bank Annuities for my use & I have cancelled the receipts. Pray receive the dividend when it is due. We have kept the wines both red & white & they are good. I have ordered £25 to you, wch. I hope you will soon receive & desire you will give the man a receipt in full on my account. My son joins with me in our service & respects & thanks for this & all favours, & I am Sir! /

Your obliged humble serv^t.
E.P.

P.S. Since I concluded this, have received your kind present of sturgeon for which I return many thanks.

For /
   Mr Moulson
     in London.

170. H.P. to Peter Moulson

Shalstone,
March the 4th, 1749.

Sir! /

I am favoured with yours of the 1st instant, & we are not willing to put our money into any of the Funds that will not be a security for 4 per cent interest certain – if you can place it out in any of the Public Funds in that manner, we shall take it as a favour if you will do so. Since your last, we have enquired & heard of a copyhold estate that we think will pay that interest. In case you judge we can have 4 p. cent int. in the Public Funds, if this is not sufficient authority to buy, we will send you one, & with both our compliments I am with due regard Sir!

Your very humble servant
H.P.

For /
   Mr Moulson . . .
     in London.

171. H.P. to Peter Moulson

Shalstone,
March the 11th, 1749.

Sir! /

I am favoured with yours dated 1st of this March, & had answered it sooner had I not had the particulars of a copyhold estate, wch. I thought to have purchased, but it does not answer so [I] desire you to subscribe our annuities according to the permits inclosed. But in case the subscribing books are shut up, then I don't question but you will do it as though it was for yourself. But I desire it may not be in any of the Insurances, because Mr Wentworth tells me he has lost considerably by embarking in those affairs. But in case you don't think it proper to sell it, nor can't subscribe it, you may let it lie where it is for the present. We both join in our compliments to you, and I am with due respect, Sir!

Your very humble serv^{t.}
H.P.

For /
     Mr Moulson in
        London.

6

The Purefoys and their Servants

THE running of an eighteenth century household was in theory a relatively easy business. Among the Purefoy papers is an explicit description of the manner in which the various functions of the household were divided up among the staff. It carries the general heading 'Of Hiring Servants & Their Particular Business'. The document is too long to quote in full, but the following catalogue of the kitchen maid's duties is typical:

'*The Cook Maid*
To roast & boil butcher's meat & all manner of fowls.
To clean all the rooms below stairs.
To make the servants beds & to clean all the garrets.
To clean the great & little stairs.
To scour the pewter & brass.
To help wash, soap & buck.
Or to do anything she is ordered.
If she has never had the smallpox to sign a paper to leave the service if she has them.'

Here was a neat compartmentalized world, which should, on paper at least, have run smoothly and without hindrance.

The methods of establishing contact between available labour and prospective employers were also formally laid down. Servants came to the

K

Purefoys either by way of recommendation from neighbours or friends, or through the open market at 'the Statute fair' held every autumn. Contracts were normally entered into for a year in the first instance, and the following extract from the account books for 1 March 1741 is not untypical: 'Hired Mary Blake then for a year from 27th of last February for the wages of three pounds & ten shillings, & gave her half a crown earnest in the presence of my son Purefoy & in his study.' This should have been a reasonably flexible system, leaving both employer and employee with considerable scope for choice. In fact, however, as the following selection of letters suggests, relations with their servants were often infinitely troublesome and embarrassing to the Purefoys.

There was first of all the difficulty of finding suitable people (Letter 181). The efficient circulation of references and recommendations between the employing classes was the only guarantee available in this respect, and the Purefoys clearly depended on these contacts. Otherwise, having clothed and fed a given servant (Letters 191 or 196), they might find him leaving their employment or simply absconding. Even with such references, however, the Purefoys had to deal with theft (Letters 173–4), absenteeism (186) and unwanted and unexpected pregnancies (182 and 185). Not surprisingly, M[rs] Purefoy developed a preference for servants who were not possessed of 'too great an assurance' (190), or who were comfortably into middle age (198). Young girls of uncertain character from other parts of the country were clearly a risk of considerable proportions.

If reliable servants were hard to find, therefore, it was wise to treat those of proven value with great consideration. The care and interest, which Henry Purefoy manifested as a trustee under the will of his former nurse, is indicative of this point (184). The Hobcraft family had served the Purefoys in many capacities in the preceding half-century, and the claims founded on such service were duly acknowledged. Even so, the letters make it plain over and over again that the turnover of staff in the Purefoy household was very rapid. M[rs] Purefoy repeatedly has to appeal to neighbours for help, in order to overcome short-term emergencies, and occasionally there was the kind of complete breakdown described in Letter 199. Even if M[rs] Purefoy's strong character made her far from the most easy-going of employers, the evidence from the letters in this section suggests that those living below stairs had ways of retaliating. As long as a good servant was as rare as a good tenant, the advantage could never lie wholly one way.

172. H.P. to William Gunn

Shalstone
Saturday, February the 21st, 1735.

William Gunn /

I am about to build a servants hall[1] which as I compute will take up 45 loads of stone, if you have a mind to undertake to build it, you must come over here the beginning of next week to treat abt it, wch will oblige

Your friend to serve you
H.P.

For /
William Gunn a mason
at Buckingham &c.

173. H.P. to Timothy Harris

Shalstone,
Sunday, January the 2nd, 1736.

Sir! /

When you granted me a warrant against Hannah Linnee,[2] you mentioned Siresham in hundred of Towcester, whereas it is in Sutton hundred. We took her last night at her mother's in Wappenham parish which is in Sutton hundred, so I am afraid the warrant is no good. I entreat you therefore to let the bearer have another warrant against Hannah Linnee to apprehend her at Wappenham or anywhere else in Sutton hundred, & the Constable to give my mother notice etc if you think proper, & let it dated as yesterday & directed to the Constable of Wappenham or any other Constable within the hundred. They did not know last night but the warrant was good, so I hope they have her still in custody. She declares she will go before Mr Sayer tomorrow. But I will order the servants to call at his house before he goes to Wappenham.

I am Sir! with real esteem.
Your very hle servt.
H.P.

For / Timothy Harris Esq
at Brackley
This.

---

1 These new quarters were completed in the autumn of 1737.
2 The maidservant in question was accused by the Purefoys of stealing beer.

174. H.P. to John Welchman

Shalstone,
January 5th, 1736.

Sir! /

On Monday last Hannah Linnee came over here with Goodman Jones of Wappenham & others. At Jones's intercession, I (unknown to my mother) agreed with her to take a guinea, so if Hannah Linnee offers you a guinea, accept it & you may then assure her from me no further prosecution shall be had against her by reason of taking the strong beer, provided she is secret & says nothing of it to anybody yet awhile. Mary Davis's friends are to come here this week wch. pray don't let Hannah Linnee know, & if she should desire to see this letter or have it to keep, don't let her for I would not have it seen under my hand that I am concerned in such an affair as this. My mother joins in our service & respect to yourself & family & I am

Your very humble servant
H.P.

P.S. Pray favour me with a line or two by Jemmy Paine on Friday next.
For /

Mr Welchman Senior at Brackley
This.

175. E.P. to Mr Sayer

Shalstone,
March the 19th, 1736.

Mr Sayer /

I want half an hundred of strong cheese for servants eating. If you have any, pray let me know by the bearer & the price wch. will oblige

Your friend to serve you
E.P.

For /

Mr Sayer jun^{r.} a Tallow Chandler
at Buckingham / This.

P.S. Let the odd ten pounds of candles be rush lights.

176. E.P. to Mr King

Shalstone,
Septembr 22nd, 1736.

Mr King /
I want a cook maid. If you should hear of any that are at the Statute[1] today, I shall be there by & by.

Your friend to serve you
E.P.

For / Mr King Senr.
a Butcher at Brackley
This d.

177. E.P. to Susannah Butler

Shalstone,
November the 11th, 1736.

Susannah Butler /
My maid Betty Huscott is gone from me. So I desire you will come over if you are not provided, according to our bargain for four pounds for a year & am

Your friend to serve you
E.P.

For / Susannah Butler
at Fritwell.
To be left at Mr Pidenton's
at Brackley

178. H.P. to Henry Sayer

Shalstone,
November the 19th, 1736.

Sir! /
I entreat the favour of you to send warrants to apprehend the four following persons (vizt),

---

1 In most country towns, a market day was set aside in the autumn for the hiring of labour of all kinds. Domestic servants and farmworkers usually contracted for one year's work, leaving open the option of changing their employer at the next Statute day.

One for Hannah Linnee of Siresham, widow, who is gone off to Padbury in this county & that must be directed to the Constable of Padbury.

Another warrant to apprehend John Jones of Buckingham, carpenter.

Another warrant for Susannah Penell, widow, of Shalstone.

Another warrant for Mary Davis of Towcester, spinster. These four have been concerned in opening the cellar door & stealing stale beer & other things. I desire you will be private in it for Hannah Linnee is so scandalous as to say that you advised her to go off to baulk the warrant. If it suits your conveniency, pray let the warrants be to appear before you some time on Monday next, or if this should not meet with you at home, let it be on Tuesday next. I am, Sir!

Your very humble serv[t.]
H.P.

For /

Henry Sayer Esq. at
Bridlesden /
This.

P.S. Since I wrote this, I am informed Hannah Linnee is gone to Adstock, so if it can be, let your warrant be so as to take Hannah Linnee anywhere in the county of Bucks, or if not so then to take her either in Shalstone, Adstock or Padbury.

179. E.P. to Thomas Robotham

Shalstone,
April the 3[d], 1737.

... And I desire you will have the following Advertizem[t.] advertized in the Saint James's Evening Post for three times. We have had our stale beer cellar door broke open & have lost between four and five hogsheads of stale beer ...

Your humble serv[t.]
E.P.

The Advertizement for the Saint James's Evening Post.

Whereas a Justice of Peace's warrant was issued out on the 19th of January last for the apprehending Mary Davis, daughter in law to M[r] Rooker of

Tossiter in the County of Northampton and late servant to Mrs Elizabeth Purefoy of Shalstone in the County of Bucks for taking and conveying away strong beer out of the cellar of the said Elizabeth Purefoy and for other misdemeanours. And whereas the said Mary Davis absconds from justice, this is to give notice that if any person or persons will discover where the said Mary Davis is, so as she may be apprehended and brought to justice as aforesaid, [they] shall receive a guinea reward from the said Elizabeth Purefoy.

For /
    Mr Robotham . . .
      London.

180. E.P. to Thomas Robotham

Shalstone,
Sunday, April 17th, 1737.

I admire Mr Read should refuse to advertize the paper I sent him, for if I had no evidence against the wench & had not the Justice's warrant by me, I should not have run the risk of doing myself a prejudice. Therefore let him advertize this advertizement I send now forthwith.

Pray desire Mrs Robotham to send me word what are the newest fashioned hats the ladies wear . . .

Your humble serv^t.
E.P.

For Mr Robotham . . .
P.S. /
    Whereas a warrant hath been lately issued out by Timothy Harris Esquire, one of His Maties Justices of the Peace for the County of North'ton, for the apprehending Mary Davis, daughter in law to Mr Rooker of Tossiter in the County aforesaid, upon oath for her taking and conveying away strong beer out of the cellar of her late Mistress Elizabeth Purefoy of Shalstone in the County of Bucks. and for other misdemeanours, and whereas the said Mary Davis absconds from justice, this is to give notice that, if any person or persons will discover where the said Mary Davis is so as she may be apprehended and brought to justice as aforesaid, [they] shall receive a guinea reward from the said Elizabeth Purefoy.

181. E.P. to William Holloway

Shalstone,
March the 21st, 1738.

William /

Thomas Esom is come, but has an ague which I hope will soon go of [f]. I want a footman to work in the garden, lay the cloath, wait at table, & to go to cart with Thomas when he is ordered, or do any other business he is ordered to do, and not too large sized a man that he may not be too great a load for an horse when he rides. He must have a good character. He only goes to cart now & then. If you hear of any such an one you may send him over. With my service to your wife, I am

Your friend to serve you
E.P.

For /

Mr William Holloway
Great Boreton . . .

182. E.P. to Mrs Sarah Dalby

Shalstone,
May the 3d, 1738.

Dear Sally /

'Tis not my dairy maid that is with child but my cookmaid, and it is reported our parson's maid is also with kinchen by the same person who has gone off & showed them a pair of heels for it. If you could help me to a cookmaid as I may be delivered from this, it will much oblige

Your affect: Godmother
& hîle servt.
E.P.

P.S. Our service is with Mrs Dalby
For /

Mrs Sarah Dalby junior at Fewcott /
This.
To be left with Mr Dodwell Colegrave
a Souldern Butcher
Carriage paid two pence.

183. E.P. to Lady Long

Shalstone,
June the 13th, 1738.

I received Lady Long's tre, & as to John Buckingham he served me 2
years and behaved soberly & honestly, & was willing & apt to do anything
I ordered him. I can spake this more knowingly, for he was entrusted here
to receive & pay for most things that came into the House, & was very
trusty tho' he could not write & I did write the receipts myself, & am
Your Ladyship's very
humble servant
E.P.

For /
The Lady Long in
Hollis Street near
Cavendish Square
London /

184. E.P. to Mrs Alice Paddon[1]

Shalstone,
Octobr the 29th, 1738.

I reced Mrs Paddon's letter together with the straw hat which I paid the
bearer 3s 6d for. My son did not then know where Mr Allestree lived, but
has since enquired & you must direct for – Allestree Esq at Birmingham in
Warwickshire by London, for he lives at Birmingham with his mother.
As to your mother, she is gone from her house at Shalstone & is still at
your brother William's at Finmere. He would have had the house set to
your Uncle John, but Nurse would not consent to it. When she went
first, I suppose she did not design to tarry at Finmere because she never came
to take her leave of me. Mrs Paxton is not come again nor I suppose never
will. Your brother William grumbled at the wood they burnt.

---

1 Alice Paddon was the married daughter of Henry Purefoy's former nurse, in whose
family he took a sedulous and benevolent interest. See also Letter 188.

If you should have occasion to come into this country, you & Mr Paddon shall be very welcome to our house during your stay here. My son & self join in service to you both wch concludes me.

Your humble serv^t
E.P.

For /

Mrs Alice Paddon at Holton
     near Dunstable in Bedfordshire by London.
P.S. Goodm^n Strange told me he would pay your mother the £20.

185. E.P. to Mr Coleman

Shalstone,
March the 3rd, 1739.

Master Coleman /

About 6 weeks ago, I hired one Deborah Coleman who tells me you are her father.

I am sorry to tell you that she is very forward with child. She denied it, and I was forced to have a midwife to search her, upon which she confessed it was so, and by Mr Launder's manservant whom she lived with.

I thought it my duty to acquaint you of it that you may take what measures you think proper. I hope you will be here today or tomorrow at farthest to take care of her. She was not willing I should send you word, but I could not omit doing it for fear it might be attended with further inconvenience, for I had a servant laid in in the house last year, and it was by chance she had not murdered the child. I am

Your unknown friend to serve you
E.P.

For /

Mr Coleman at
     Launton /
          This.

186. E.P. to Henry Stanbridge

Shalstone,
August 12th, 1741.

Master Stanbridge /

'Tis now above six weeks since your daughter went from Shalstone & we have heard nothing from her since. She told a charwoman, who works here sometimes, she would give her anything she would have if she would do the work till she came again. This charwoman demands great pay, and we had a servant girl gone away since Martha went, who has not behaved as honest as she should do, & as Martha has left her clothes here littering about, & we not knowing what she has, she may loose something tho' we have taken what care we can.

I think it very careless in not sending before this time. Pray let us hear from you forthwith, wch. will oblige

Your friend to serve you.

E.P.

For /
> Mr Henry Stanbridge Senior
>> at Bicester /
>>> This.

Carriage paid 2 pence.

187. H.P. to Mr Johnson

Shalstone,

Novemb^r. the 24th, 1741.

Mr Johnson /

I desire you will make Kirton Gostello a black cap of bastard velvet, the same bigness in the head with your son John, & he will meet you at Brackley old fair if you bring it with you & pay you five shillings (wch he says) is the price of it – He says you made him some while he lived with Mr Cave of Eydon much to his satisfaction. I am

Yours in haste

H.P.

For /
> Mr Johnson & Taylor
>> at Culworth /
>>> This d.

Carriage paid two pence.

188. H.P. to Thomas Paddon

Shalstone,

June the 20th, 1742.

Mr Paddon /

I should have been glad to have seen you & Mrs Paddon according to your word the next day after you was with us, that you might have given me a note for the twenty pounds you owed my late Nurse Hobcraft. You know I am mentioned a trustee in her will for this twenty pounds. I am resolved to see my late Nurse's will fulfilled to the utmost of my power, therefore I expect you should sign a note acknowledging you owe the said twenty pounds, & the same to be payable or answerable to such purposes as the will directs. I called on your brother Hobcraft at Finmere to know whether he should go your way & when, & he said he thought sometime about next Michas.

I propose to get a proper note drawn against that time for your perusal & for you to sign, wch. I intend to send by your brother Hobcraft. Pray let me have your answer soon per post, whether I should send it by him or no. With our service & respects to yourself & Mrs Paddon, I am

Your humble serv^t
H.P.

For /
    Mr Thomas Paddon
        a schoolmaster at Houghton
            near Dunstable
                Bedfordshire.
By way of London

189. E.P. to Mrs Mary Sheppard

Shalstone,
Feb^{ry.} 23th, 1743.

I rece^d Mrs Sheppard's letter. I hope the maid will do if she can sew well, that is to work fine plain work as mobs & ruffles. If she comes, she must bring a character of her honesty from the person she lived with last. My custom is to give the servants a shilling for horse hire & they come themselves, & I will give her half a crown because she comes so far. If she agrees to this, she may come next Wednesday or next Thursday. The horse & man who attend her shall be welcome to stay here all night, & shall be glad to see you here when fine weather comes. If I don't see her here by Thursday next, I shall conclude she will not come at all. I am

Your friend to serve you
E.P.

P.S. / Your son presents his duty to you. He has but 4 shirts to wear & desires you would send him two shirts when the maid comes. The sleeves must be very near half an ell long.

For / Mrs Mary Sheppard at
   Cornewall near Chipping Norton
     in
        Oxfordshire.
   By way of London

190. E.P. to John Whitmore

Shalstone,
March the 16th, 1743.

I received Mr Whitmore's letter & am obliged to you for enquiring after a maid, & if her living at home in a public house has not given her too great an assurance to live in a civilized private family, I think there will be a probability of her doing, & you may send her over. I thank you for buying my meat, & desire you will buy me next week a good hind quarter of veal.
                  This will oblige
                  Your friend to serve you
                  E.P.

For /
   Mr John Whitmore
     at Brackley.
      This.

191. H.P. to Mr Fell

Shalstone
Sunday, 17th June, 1744.

Mr Fell /
   I desire you will come over here either on Wednesday or Thursday next, & the men shall be in the way for you to measure them for their liveries – bring some patterns of green cloth & of serge Paduasa[1] & patterns of brass

---

1 Paduasoy or Paduasa was a strong, hard-wearing fabric in corded silk.

buttons – don't fail coming then for they must be made up by the 7th of July to be at Buckingham Assize – I am

Your friend to serve you
H.P.

P.S. Bring a yard and a half of shalloon[1] the same colour of the pattern of cloth enclosed.

For /

Mr Fell senr. at Chipping Norton.

192. E.P. to Mrs E. Barrett

Shalstone,
October the 3rd, 1744.

I desire Miss Betty & Mr Wallbank to enquire me out a cookmaid – The same wench who disappointed me last year has disappointed me again. She took half a crown earnest & three days after sent it again – if you hear of any, pray send her over which will oblige

Your humble servant
E.P.

For / Mrs Elizabeth Barrett at Mr Wallbank's at Buckingham.

193. E.P. to Mrs Wallbank

Shalstone,
Octobr. 14th, 1744.

Sir! /

I reced your letter, and Baldwin says Hester Gibbard understands a dairy as well as dressing of meat; if she comes here, she must milk & manage the dairy of 2 or 3 cows as well as the cooking, and if she complies with this she may come over. My maid Baldwin has given me notice 4 or 5 times to go away, & is resolved to leave me, she says as soon as our next washing is over, wch. is this week. I tell her she shall go when I can provide myself. If you or Miss Bett. hear of one for her place, it will be a favour if you will

---

1 A closely woven woollen material chiefly used for linings.

let me know, for she is so violent spirited I had rather have her room than her company. With our compliments to you all, am Sir!

Your humble servant
E.P.

For /
    Mʳ Wallbank a surgeon
      at Buckingham /
      This.

194. E.P. to Mary Gee

Shalstone,
February the 19ᵗʰ, 1745.

Mary Gee

The reason I did not send for you was because you told me the last place you lived at was with a gentlewoman & that you lived with her four years. I hear you have lived since Michaelmas at one Master Smith's of Chackmore & that you have been at two other places since Michaelmas. The reason I part with my present cookmaid is her telling falsities. I am afraid by this you are indicted to the same; there is no such thing as living with me unless you are endued with downright truth, & assure yourself if you do come here, I will write to the gentlewoman for a character of you. The bearer hereof will bring you in his wagon in case you can clear yourself in this affair & think you can do the business, if not pray stay where you are, from

Your friend to serve you
E.P.

For /
    Mary Gee at the Widow
      Gee's at Farthingoe
      This.

195. E.P. to Mrs Mary Blake

Shalstone
Monday, Septr· the 23ᵗʰ, 1745.

This is to desire Mary Blake to enquire after the gardiner's son you used to talk of, who had a mind to come to service; if he now wants a place, I want a servant to look after the garden, & upon occasion to wait at table, but his chief business will be in the garden, for I keep a coachman & footman besides. If he can't come over, I will come to Bicester to him, if you will let me know what day by Mr. Rawlins the butcher of Heath, & if you know of ever a maid for your place, send her over or let me know for my maid is lame. Pray my son's & my service to your brother, I am

Your friend to serve you
E.P.

For /
    Mrs Mary Blake at M^r
       Woodfield's, a mercer at
         Bicester /
           This.

196. E.P. to Mr Yates

Shalstone,
March the 22th, 1748.

Mr Yates /
    I desire you will chose me from your son's a quarter of an hundred or half an hundred weight of good strong cheese for the servants, such as Goodman Franklin of Shalstone had of him last Wednesday. I don't care how small sized the cheeses be. I think you don't sell cheese yourself; let me know the price by the bearer & then I will send for them who am

Your friend to serve you
E.P.

For /
    Mr Yates senior at Brackley
       This.

197. E.P. to Mrs Priscilla Higgins

Shalstone,
October the 19th, 1748.

Priscilla Higgins /
    The Revd. Mr William Fletcher was here on Monday last, and informs me that your mother desired him to get a place in a gentleman's family,

she being uneasy that you were in a public house & that you had set yourself
for a month only, so that if you think proper to accept of my place, you know
my business & I will give you four pounds a year wages. Pray let me have
your answer by the bearer. From

Your friend to serve you
E.P.

For /
    Mrs Priscilla Higgins
       at the Crosskeys Inn at
       Buckingham

198. E.P. to Mr Watts

Shalstone
Wednesday, Feb^{ry} 21st, 1749.

Mr Watts /

    I want a maid in my maid Hannah's place, if you should hear of ever a
one whom you think is fit for the place. She must sew plain work, wash
fine linen & iron, & to help to send in dinner on extraordinary days. I
should like her never the worse if she was forty years old. If it lies in your
way to assist me in this affair, I desire you will send one over, & am

Your friend to serve you
E.P.

For /
    Mr Watts a Tailor at
       Whitfield
       This.

199. H.P. to Peter Moulson

Shalstone,
August the 16th, 1753.

Sir! /

    I am favoured with yours dated the 3^{d.} of July last, & am much obliged
to you for your kind invitation. I should be glad to accept it & should
endeavour to make a suitable return, but at present my coachman is run

L

away from me for fear of a great belly a girl lays to him,[1] & our cookmaid was forced to go to Oxford Assize to be evidence against a felon there, & when she came home she said she was married, & our gardiner has married my mother's maid, & we have had a very valuable mare lamed with a fork but now in a fair way of recovery, so our little family is in a state of confusion at present. However, if we can't come to Town, I hope we shall see you & Mr & Mrs Vaughan & George the Second[2] here. The Birmingham coach runs thro' in a day from London to Buckingham, & the fare is ten shillings each passenger, & if you let us know when you will come our chariot shall meet you at Buckingham . . . & I am with all due esteem, Sir!

Your very humble servt.
H.P.

For /
    Mr Moulson in
      London /
        This.

---

[1] In such cases as this, paternity was simply established on the mother's word. This naturally gave pregnant girls considerable opportunities for blackmail.

[2] Since Vaughan's Christian name was also George, it became a standing joke in the Purefoy family to call his son George the Second after the reigning monarch.

7

Leisure

ONE of the principal problems of county life in the eighteenth century was its unutterable tediousness. A spell of bad weather could cut off communities completely, and most forms of social life were conditioned by finding suitable companions. This chapter describes the two main sources of amusement open to men of Henry Purefoy's standing.

Purlieu hunting was clearly a great occasion for the Purefoy family and their neighbours. The purlieus were those tracts of land, which, now disafforested, once formed part of the royal forests, and over which the laws relating to those forests still held sway. Naturally, it was easy to dispute that certain areas of land came within the purlieus, and if the memory of the oldest men failed on a given issue, the only possible recourse was to shift the argument to a perusal of old maps and charters (Letter 205). Henry Purefoy's contretemps with the Dukes of Bridgwater (Letter 204) and Grafton (Letter 206) clearly suggest that even a simple taste for hare coursing could involve the unsuspecting in legal traps and entanglements. The fact that the assistance of the local M.P. had to be called upon emphasizes the seriousness with which such rights were guarded.

Henry Purefoy too took hunting seriously. The account books and diaries confirm that he spent considerable sums on horses and dogs, and that he could always be considered a likely buyer for any animal of this kind with reputed promise. Equally clearly, his ability to issue an invitation to his friends to come hunting on his ground was a matter of great pride and selectively exercised. The whole outing would be spoilt if the meet was too crowded (Letter 203).

For obvious reasons though, this form of activity was vulnerable to bad weather, failing light and the vagaries of the game. All these factors pointed to the necessity of having other outlets for relaxation. Sermons and the dispensation of local justice had entertainment possibilities, but clearly of a limited kind. More fundamental was the Purefoy emphasis on reading. The surviving letters to booksellers are grouped together in the second half of this chapter, and demonstrate quite firmly that Macaulay's description of the eighteenth century squire as a brutish, uncouth drunkard is here very wide of the mark. The taking of the *Gentleman's Magazine* was the lowest common denominator of polite society. It offered the minimum that was felt necessary of national and international news, together with specialist articles on all subjects, and births, marriages and deaths. The Purefoys clearly went beyond this, however, as the orders for history, classical authors and the printed Acts of Parliament suggest. This was a very literate family, who wished to be kept up to date with political events at all levels.

Although this final chapter is, in some senses, not as immediately interesting as its predecessors, it should not be too easily dismissed or glossed over. In fact it contains good evidence that the type of county society represented by the Purefoys was as hard-riding as has been supposed, but that it also hoped to explore areas of experience for which some historians have denied them all credit.

(a) HUNTING

200. H.P. to Edward Trotman[1]

Shalstone,
Thursday, 11th January, 1738.

Sir! /

Our little black bitch Chloe goes to heat & you was so kind to promise me your least dog hound to ward her, so I have sent the servant for him. He shall be taken the utmost care of and returned to you again safe in 2 or 3 days. We were in hopes of waiting on you & Mrs Trotman at Shalstone before now, & with our compliments for the season I am, Sir!

Your very humble serv^t.
H.P.

---

[1] The Trotman family, who bought the Shelswell estate in 1720, were close friends of the Purefoys, and visiting between the two families was on a regular basis.

For /
    Edward Trotman Esq at
      Shellswell /
        This.

201. H.P. to the Rev Thomas Price

                                Sept^r· the 29th, 1739.
Sir! /
    My man Thomas Chandler acquaints me that you took an hare out of
the mouth of my greyhounds in Shalstone Cowpasture on Thursday last
in the afternoon, and would not deliver it to him tho' he asked you for it.
As the hare was caught by my own greyhounds & on my own ground, I
look upon it to be my property. It disappointed me from sending it to
London as today, so I desire you will deliver it to the bearer. I am
                        Your humble serv^t·
                            H.P.

For /
    The Rev^d· M^r· Thos· Price
      at Buckingham /
        This.

202. E.P. to Thomas Robotham

                    Shalstone,
                    Tuesday, Septemb^r· the 14th, 1742.

    This acquaints Mr Robotham we are come to Shalstone, & shall be
glad to see you here as soon as may be, the coursing season being in the prime;
with our best service & wishes for yours & Mrs Robothams health, am in
haste
                      Your ĥle servant
                        E.P.

For / Mr Robotham at the
    King's Head against the Church
      in Islington near
        London

203. H.P. to Mr Garland

Shalstone,
August the 5th, 1748.

Mr Garland /

I shall go on purlieu hunting tomorrow morning, & should be glad to meet you at Siresham Hatch about six o'clock in the morning or sooner. Pray bring no dogs with you, but what are fit for the purpose, & don't mention anything of our going to anybody least it should take wind & hinder our sport. I am

Your humble serv^{t.}
H.P.

For /
      Mr Garland at
         Brackley
            This.

204. H.P. to John Wodhull

Shalstone,
Septemb^{r.} the [20th], 1750.

Sir! /

The occasion of this trouble from me is – I was lately discharged from purlieu hunting in all the Duke of Bridgwater's woods by their woodward Garland, an innholder of Brackley, on which, thinking myself under an hardship, I had a case drawn up by an attorney to know how far the rights of the owners of the purlieu woods extended in relation to their mutually hunting in each other's woods, – wch. case now lies before Councellor Willis (son to the Ld. Chief Justice). But he informs me that the general law is very clear on this point, but before he can answer my case he must know the particular customs of our hunting in each other's purlieu woods. I was yesterday to wait on our good neighbour Mr Wentworth, but he could not resolve me sufficiently, but recommended me to you as very knowing & intelligent in this affair. What I would entreat to know of you is whether the constant practice has been for the purlieu men to hunt & kill deer & climb up the trees for that purpose in each other's woods as well as their own woods; & if the deer we rouse in our own woods should escape

into those of our neighbours' woods, whether we can't pursue 'em into our
neighbours' woods & justify getting up in trees to shoot 'em, & in what
case we may set our reels or long strings with feathers to 'em to awe &
keep the deer within the woods, & if there have been any p'secutions of the
owners of purlieu woods against any or each other for hunting deer in each
other's purlieu woods in your remembrance. If you please to favour me
with an answer hereto by the bearer & to excuse this freedom, it will much
oblige, S^r.

Your very humble servant
H.P.

P.S. My mother joins with me in our compliments to you & Mrs Wodull.
To /

   John Wodull Esq
      at Thenford /
         This.

205. H.P. to Edward Willes[1]

Shalstone,
Septemb^{r.} the 25th, 1750.

Sir! /

Since I had the pleasure of waiting on you at Astrop, I have paid a visit
to my good neighbour Mr Wentworth who is 70 & odd years of age &
has been a purlieu man these 50 years past, & he informs me that he being
no sportsman himself, his servants have all along roused & hunted the deer
in his own woods & Mr Dayrell's & Mr Hosier's & other gentlemen's
woods on that side Whittlebury Forest, & got up the trees & shot deer in
these other woods as well as in his own, & that these other gentlemen have
took the same liberty in his woods for that space of time without any
interruption on either side. But he says, as there was always a good understanding & good neighbourhood between himself & these other gentlemen,
this freedom & forbearance on either side may be imputed to these occasions,
but that in his opinion they can't strictly rouse deer nor get up in trees in
another man's woods, but that they may hunt the deer roused in their own

---

1 Edward Willes: was called to the Bar in 1747 and became a Judge in the Court of
  King's Bench in 1767. He was M.P. for Aylesbury from 1747 to 1754. On all grounds
  therefore, he was an ideal person to give advice and assistance on this particular problem.

woods thro' any other's woods or shoot 'em there. Besides this, I wrote a letter to Mr Wodull of Thenford whose answer to my queries I send you inclosed. This is all the light I can procure you in this affair, & I am with all due respect, Sir! /

Your most humble servant
H.P.

For /
    Edward Wills Esquire
        Member of Parliament at
            Mr Morgan's Coffeehouse
                in Bath, Somersetshire /
            By London /
               Frank.

206. H.P. to Peter Moulson

Shalstone,
Octob{r.} the 18th, 1750.

Sir! /

    I am favoured with yours of the 16th of this instant October, & have this morning sent for the mountain wine with orders to put this in the post, for yesterday at Brackley market I heard by a lawyer that my Lord Duke of Grafton[1] had ordered a case to be laid before the Attorney General to question my right of hunting in the purlieus, &, in case he did not judge me to have a right to hunt in the purlieus, to file an information against me for killing deer. As my father & ancestors have always hunted in the purlieus without interruption, I have done the same within these four or five years, and I am not conscious to myself of having ever trespassed on the forest in any one shape. If his Grace designs to call my right of hunting in the purlieus in question, I must beg the favour of him not to file an information against me immediately, but to give me leave to lay before him my case, wherein shall be contained my right & title to hunt in the purlieus & then to condescend to let me have his answer whether he approves it or no.

    If you nor any friend of yours can't come to speak with his Grace, I have

---

[1] Charles Fitzroy, 2nd Duke of Grafton (1683–1757). He was characterized by Swift 'as almost a slobberer'. Certainly, he took little part in public affairs, preferring to indulge a passion for hunting. He died after falling off a horse.

enclosed a letter wch. I desire you will seal it & let it be conveyed to his hands as soon as possible, for the term[1] begins the 23rd. of this month, but if you think you can secure my interest in the affair without delivering the letter you may lay it by.

We are heartily sorry to hear you are ill & wish your speedy recovery, & hope George the Second will live with his Mama to be a comfort to her & Mr Vaughan, for I myself could not speak till I was 2 years old. My mother joins with me in our compliments & desiring you to excuse this trouble, am with due esteem Sir!

Your very humble servant
H.P.

P.S. This matter is the more surprizing to me as I never heard the Duke was displeased [with] me till lately. Sure I am I would have waited on his Grace about it had I known of it when he had been in the country.

207. H.P. to the Duke of Grafton

Shalstone,
Octob^{r.} the 18th, 1750.

My Lord Duke /

I am informed that I am so unhappy as to have fallen under your Grace's displeasure on account of having killed a deer on Whittlebury Forest ground, which upon honour I never did, and that you imagine I have no right to hunt in the purlieus. My father & our ancestors before him have always hunted in the purlieus without interruption, & for myself I have only followed their example for four or five years past; and I entreat the favour you will give me leave to lay before your Grace my right & title to hunt in the purlieus, for I hear you design to apply to the Attorney General to have an information filed against me on account of this affair, wch. will be very hard on me if you do so, by reason not any one gentleman in the Forest gave me the least intimation that you was offended with me. If I had heard anything of it, I would have waited on your Grace when you was in this country in order to have cleared myself, wch. I hope you will still give me leave to do, & not to proceed against me till you have seen my case,

---

1 The legal term.

& have honoured me with your answer thereto, & that you will be assured
that I am with all due esteem,

Your Grace's most obedient and

most humble servant.

H.P.

To /

    His Grace the Duke

      of Grafton

        Humbly present.

208. H.P. to Browne Willis

Shalstone,

October the 18th, 1750.

Sir! /

My Lord Duke of Grafton (as I am informed) has ordered his lawyer to
lay a case before the Attorney General in order to have an information filed
against me by him for killing deer in the purlieus, as not being a lawful
purlieu man. My father & ancestors always hunted in the purlieus & their
right was never called in Quẽõn, & as I claim under him and them I look
on myself to be a legal purlieu man. The old men in this parish say there
were 250 acres & upwards of my ground that were disafforested & name the
very place (to wit) Dickens's hedge, where the bounds of the forest ended.
This should seem to prove that Shalstone is one of the Forest Towns,[1]
but how to prove it so unless it be by Domesday Book or some ancient
records I cannot tell, so entreat the favour of you to let me know as soon as
may be what records & where I must search on this occasion. It would be
exceeding kind of you if you would call & take a commons[2] with us as
you come from Aynhoe, then you might favour me with instructions etc,
for the term begins the 23[rd] of this month & then they may begin against
me. But if your leisure will not permit you to favour me with your company,
I must entreat the favour of a line or two to be left for me at M[r] Wallbank's
at Buckingham, & with my mother's compliments am Sir!, in haste

Your obliged h[l]e servant

H.P.

---

[1] A town which had grown up on the site of a former royal forest.

[2] Commons; common meal.

For /
   Dr Willis /
      This.

209. H.P. to John Pollard

Shalstone,
Novembr. the 4th, 1750.

Sir! /

Our worthy friend Dr. Brown Willis does me the favour to dine with me at your County Town of Bucks tomorrow, & intends to call on you as he goes by to look into Manwood's Forest Laws, if you have it by you, in behalf of me who am threatened by his Grace the Duke of Grafton abt. the purlieu hunting. If it should not suit with your convenience to be at home, pray leave this book out if you have it for the Doctor to look on, which will much oblige Sir!

Your very hle servant
H.P.

P.S. My mother & my complimts. wait
    on Mrs Pollard & yourself.

For /
   John Pollard Esqre.
     at Finmere /
       This.

210. H.P. to Peter Moulson

Shalstone,
November the 6th, 1750.

Sir! /

I am favoured with yours of the 3d. instant, & desire your acceptance of my hearty thanks for your kind endeavours to serve me. But whilst my Lord Duke of Grafton has such generous intentions of ordering me a brace of bucks, Mr Smith of Shelbrook Lodge & the other foresters are prosecuting me & my friends here with uncommon fury, for there is one Mr Joseph Harris, a bankrupt & a man of a very indifferent character, has made information on oath that one Wm. Collison, a mason, with four other men who were hunting with me, killed a deer on & took of[f] from the Forest ground on the 15th of August last. As to the ground, it was half a mile from the Forest pales, but whether belonging to the Forest or no I can't tell. The deer lay in the ditch & the head & the legs on the bank, & the dogs with the deer & no soul with them. Then two of the men came & the deer was dead. Some say 'tis Forest ground & some not. It was a very poor deer, & I would not give half a crown for it. Upon this information, Wm. Collison was apprehended & had before a Justice, & would have been sent to Northton Jail had not I & some of his friends been bound in a recognizance of £75 for his appearance at next Northampton Assizes. But the foresters were against accepting bail, so I was forced to attend again at the Sessions at Thrup where the Justices accepted the bail & Collison was set at liberty. It was a very wet day & I was wet to the skin, & at these Sessions I met Mr Smith of Shellbrook, & I asking him how he could use me so ill by prosecuting in [so] clandestine a manner without giving me any notice. He answered that he had very strict orders from my Lord Duke of Grafton to set this prosecution on foot, & to continue it till he had orders from his Grace to the contrary, & that 'twas none of his own doings, & that his Grace, as soon as he has paid his devoirs[1] to the King, will go to Euston Hall[2] & stay there till X^{t.}mas. So I must entreat the favour of you, as soon as you can after you receive this, to wait on his Grace & to entreat of him to give orders to his secretary, Mr. Modocks, to favour me with a line or two that his Grace consents that this prosecution against this Collison & others may be withdrawn, & that his Grace also consents that the recognizance we have entered into for Collison's appearance may be vacated, & Mr. Smith says if I can show him such a letter he will put an end to the prosecution. If his Grace should be gone to Euston, if you can't write to him yourself, I must entreat you to let me know what you would advise me to do, wch. will much oblige, Sir!

Your most humble servant

H.P.

P.S. My mother joins with me in our compliments to you.

For / Mr Moulson in London

---

1 Devoirs; respects.
2 The estate house of the Grafton family in Suffolk.

211. H.P. to Peter Moulson

Shalstone,
Decemb^r· the 23rd·, 1750.

Sir! /

I am favoured with yours dated 15th of last month & am much obliged to you for your kind endeavours to serve me in this affair. I am afraid we have not succeeded with the Duke because I have not heard from you. I have often sent to Shelbrook Lodge to Mr Smith but he is never at home, but I hope to meet with him there today, & wish it were made an end on for here is a sad clamour in the country about it. I should be glad to know who are my adversaries, sure I am I have never gave anybody occasion to be so in any respect, & when the deer was killed, I was half a mile of[f] from it. . .

Your obliged ħle serv^t·
H.P.

For / Mr Moulson . . .
London
With a basket, carriage paid.

212. H.P. to Lord Cobham

Shalstone,
January the 3^d·, 1750. [1751]

My Lord /

I have reced the honour of your letter dated 25th of last month, w^{ch}· I should have answered sooner but company came in upon me & prevented me. I return you abundance of thanks for your kind interposition in my behalf & beg the continuance thereof, for I am informed my Lord Duke is not yet thoroughly appeased. My mother joins with me in our desire that yourself & Lady Cobham will accept of our humble respect & the compliments of the season, & I beg you'll be assured that I am with all due esteem, my Lord.

Your L^{dsps}· most obedient &
obliged ħle servant
H.P.

For /
The right honoble the L^d· Cobham
in Pall Mall /
London.
Frank.

213. H.P. to John Wodhull

Shalstone,
March the 27ᵗʰ, 1751.

Sir! /

I have been to wait on the Duke of Grafton abᵗ· this troublesome affair. He drank my health at dinner, but when I came to desire him to withdraw his prosecution, he referred me to Mʳ· Smith of Shelbrook Lodge, who went with me to my horse & told me he should never have done anything in this affair unless I had waited on the Duke, & when I told him I would wait on him at Shellbrook about it, he told me he would call on me at Shalstone very soon, but he not coming I went on Monday last to Shellbrook, but Mʳ Smith was gone from home & Mʳˢ Smith told me he would not be at home under 4 or 5 days, so must desire you to acquaint me by the bearer whether anybody from the Duke of Grafton has been with you to withdraw the prosecution. If they have not, the recognizance (we have entered into) must be drawn & sent over on Saturday next to Northampton by your clerk or some safe hand (that being the first day of the Assizes there), & it must be delivered to the Clerk of the Assize that day, & Mʳ Collison must appear then, as I am informed, & if no prosecution he will be discharged the last day of the Assizes. I believe it will be necessary for Mʳ Collison to know where your Clerk or person you send the recognizance by inns at Northampton, that he may attend him into Coᵗ· with it, so entreat you will let me know thereof by the bearer. This has been the most troublesome affair I ever met with. My mother joins with me in our compliments to yourself & Mʳˢ Woodhull, & thanks for all favours, wishing you both the blessing of health, & I am with all due esteem Sir!

Your obliged humble servant
H.P.

For /
  John Wodhull Esq.
    at Thenford /
      This.

214. H.P. to Peter Moulson

Shalstone,
April the 9ᵗʰ, 1751.

Sir! /

I am favoured with yours, & yesterday I received the favour of a tre from Mr Smith of Shellbrook lodge intimating that his Grace condescended to make all matters easy, & I thank you & Mr Williams for your good offices in this difficult affair, wch. I am heartily glad we are rid of.

Your obliged humble serv^t.
H.P.

For /
    Mr Moulson in
       London
    post paid 3^d.

215. H.P. to Peter Moulson

Shalstone,
July the 4th, 1753.

Sir /

This morning my Lord Duke of Grafton sent me half a buck wch. was killed yesterday. I desire you to accept of an haunch of it sent carriage paid by Mr Jones our carrier who comes into Town on Fridays. My mother desires to join with me in our compliments to you & I am with due esteem, Sir! /

Your very humble servant
H.P.

For /
    Mr Moulson
      in
        London.

(6) BOOKS

216. H.P. to Mr Cooper

Shalstone,
Wednesday, March the 2nd, 1736.

Mr Cooper /

I send you by the bearer Dr Cheyne's Essay on the Gout, S^r. Walter Raleigh's Remains, Lillie's Book, & Cornaro, Rosse's View of all Religions, Balzac's Letters, & the 12 monthly Gentleman's Magazine for 1736 with the supplement thereto, all which I desire may be bound in calf. On the

back of the Magazines let there be 1736 in gilt figures, & let the binding of
that be a brown colour & smooth leather; let some of the other books be a
smooth black leather for variety, & pray send word by the bearer when I
may send for 'em again, wch. will oblige

Your friend & serv^t.

H.P.

For /
   Mr Cooper a
      Schoolmaster at
         Brackley.

217. H.P. to J. Paine

Shalstone,

May ye 3^d, 1738.

Mr Paine /

I desire you will Send for Dr Bowles's fundamentall Rules of the Latin
Grammar And the 31st Vollume of Salmons modern history (with the Maps
& the Cuts thereto) wch I am Sure is come out Because I saw it advertized.
This will oblige

Your humble Servt

H.P.

ffor / Mr Tommy Paine a
   Baker[1] at Brackley
      This d.

218. H.P. to James Payne

Shalstone,

May the 27th, 1740.

Mr Paine /

I desire you will deliver the letter & stocking to Mr Collison, & bring
from him a pair of black silk stockings & the stocking sent, & when you

---

[1] It was usual for bookselling to be a hobby of one of the tradesmen in most provincial
centres, who would undertake to order books from London. There was, however,
no necessary connection between baking and bookselling.

write to London, write for an Abstract of the Acts of Parliament passed
this last Session. This will oblige

Your humble serv^t

H.P.

For /
    Mr James Payne a
        Baker at Brackley.
            This d.

219. H.P. to James Payne

Shalstone,
January the 6th, 1747.

Mr Paine /
    The Plautus you sent me has only three of the Comedies translated,
whereas I hoped Echard had translated all his Comedies. If he has let me have
the rest of them. Hobb's Thucidides was very lately to be had at one Samuel
Birt's in Ave-Mary-Lane. I return the Terence again. It is so badly bound,
I don't care to let it have a place in my study, but desire you to get me one
that is better bound. I have received the Quintus Curtius, wch. I like very
well, & desiring you to accept of the compliments of the season, am

Your humble servant

H.P.

For /
    Mr James Paine
        at Brackley /
            This.

220. H.P. to James Payne

Shalstone,
Sunday, March the 11th, 1749.

Mr Payne,
    On the 28th of February last, I sent you a letter with an advertizement
inclosed, on which was the title of the following book (vizt·)
    The disadvantages of the Married State or the Artifices & foibles of the

M

fair sex such as in Music, Dancing, Dress, Equipage, Desire of Offspring etc considered, & the Single Life plainly proved preferable to that of Marriage.

Art thou loosed from a Wife, seek not a Wife. Who can find a virtuous Woman?

This I say is the title of the book I desired you to send for me, & instead thereof you (by mistake I suppose) have sent me a book entitled: A serious Proposal for promoting Marriage etc:, which I send you again by the bearer & desire you will return it to your bookseller. Your behaviour to me in this affair really puts me in mind of the confusion of languages at Babel, when one asked for an hammer they gave him a trowel. What I desire of you now is to write for the book as I ordered. I can't say the title of the book is verbatim, but I send you the substance of it so as to render it intelligible, & hope you won't use me so any more, nor give me any other reason than to be

Your assured friend
H.P.

For /
  Mr James Payne at
    Brackley /
      This
        With a book.

A Chronology
1714-1760

1714   Queen Anne died and was succeeded by the Elector of Hanover, who became George I.

1715   A general election resulted in a victory for the supporters of the Hanoverians (especially the Whigs). The death of Louis XIV of France and the succession of the five-year-old Louis XV (who reigned until 1774) contributed to the failure of Jacobite risings in Scotland, and northern and south-western England.

1716   In the aftermath of the rebellion parliament extended its life from 3 to 7 years, and postponed the next election from 1718 to 1722; this helped to prevent the Tories from ever regaining their pre-1714 position of power. Britain, France and Holland allied against Sweden, Spain and the Jacobites.

1717   Walpole and Townshend left Sunderland's Whig administration.

1718   The Schism Act and the Occasional Conformity Act were repealed, extending the civil rights of dissenters. Thomas Lambe patented a silk-throwing machine, which he was to employ in a Derbyshire factory.

1719   The Peerage Bill, attempting to restrict the Crown's powers of creating new peerages, was rejected by the Commons. A Spanish landing in Scotland in favour of the Jacobite cause was defeated. Defoe's *Robinson Crusoe* was published.

1720   Townshend and Walpole re-entered the Stanhope-Sunderland administration. A scheme for funding the National Debt led to a speculative mania, and the consequent failure of confidence was 'the bursting of the South Sea Bubble'.

1721   The Treaty of Nystad ended the Great Northern War between

Russia and Sweden during which Hanover had made some gains, and Britain's commercial interests in the Baltic had been for the most part protected. Lady Wortley Montague and the Princess of Wales popularized inoculation for smallpox.

1722   Walpole, who had became Chancellor of the Exchequer and First Lord of the Treasury the previous year, became leader of the administration with the death of Sunderland. Walpole reduced land tax from 3s. in the £ to 2s. in the £ in this election year. A Jacobite plot for a coup d'état failed.

1724   Swift published his anonymous Drapier's Letters attacking Wood who had a patent for minting halfpennies for Ireland.

1726   Pulteney and Bolingbroke began to edit an opposition journal, *The Craftsman*. Bolingbroke's friend Swift published *Gulliver's Travels*, including satire on Walpole.

1727   Spain blockaded Gibraltar and an undeclared war broke out. Land tax was raised to the maximum rate of 4s. in the assessed £. George II succeeded George I, and there was a general election.

1728   A shortage of corn was reflected in high prices. Walpole passed his first annual Indemnity Act, waiving the restrictions on dissenters' civil rights for twelve months. John Gray's *Beggar's Opera*, satirizing the Walpole administration, was first performed.

1730   Townshend left Walpole's ministry after advocating a more active foreign policy; he retired to Norfolk to introduce a four-course system of husbandry.

1732   Land tax was reduced to 1s. in the £; land and assessed taxes made their smallest contribution to the revenue throughout the eighteenth century in 1733 and 1734.

1733   Walpole's scheme for replacing land taxes by duties on commodities (excises) met popular opposition and was withdrawn before a parliamentary defeat should be sustained. Kay patented the flying shuttle, heightening the imbalance in productivity between hand-weavers and hand-spinners.

1734   Despite the reverse of the previous year, the Duke of Newcastle's management contributed to maintaining a majority for Walpole in the general election. Walpole held himself responsible for Britain's non-involvement in the currently raging War of Polish Succession.

1735   John Wesley started his Journals; Hogarth executed his *Rake's Progress*.

1736 The statutes against witchcraft were repealed.

1737 Frederick Prince of Wales quarrelled with his father and set up a separate establishment that became a focus of opposition. Queen Caroline, who had been an important channel for Walpole's influence over George II, died.

1738 There was pressure in parliament for war on account of Spain's enforcement of trading monopoly with its colonial empire. John Wesley underwent his evangelical conversion.

1739 After the failure of a negotiated settlement war broke out with Spain.

1740 This war was generalized after the death of the Emperor. The new King of Prussia, Frederick the Great, invaded Maria Theresa's province of Silesia, while France supported a Bavarian claim for the imperial throne against Maria Theresa's husband. Britain was involved through Hanover. Land tax was raised. Richardson's *Pamela*, sometimes accounted the first novel, was published.

1741 Walpole's majority was somewhat eroded in the general election. Handel composed his *Messiah* (first performed in 1742).

1742 Walpole resigned and became Earl of Oxford.

1743 The forces of Britain and its allies, with George II present as commander-in-chief, were luckily extricated from encirclement by victory at the Battle of Dettingen.

1744 War was formally declared between Britain and France. Britain was threatened with a French invasion.

1745 After the British defeat at Fontenoy and the virtual loss of the Austrian Netherlands, the threat of French invasion intensified. Confidence in the notes of the Bank of England was quickly restored at the end of September after the Jacobites had secured themselves in Edinburgh by the Battle of Prestonpans. An army of Highlanders penetrated to Derby in early December, but a Hanoverian royal army had been concentrated in the west midlands.

1746 A collective resignation by the Pelham administration forced George II to abandon his other advisers and take back the Pelhams along with Pitt. The Jacobites were defeated at Culloden.

1747 In a general election Henry Pelham, who had in effect been chief minister since 1743, consolidated the Walpolian Old Corps.

1748 The Wars of the Austrian Succession were terminated by the Peace of Aix-la-Chapelle. Smollet's *Roderick Random* was published.

1749 Fielding's *Tom Jones* was published.

1751 Frederick Prince of Wales died and his son became heir apparent. More effective control of illicit gin sales was introduced.

1752 By an Act of 1751 the Gregorian Calendar replaced the Julian. The New Year was reckoned officially from January 1st 1752 (whereas the previous one had been reckoned from March 25th 1751) and the days September 3rd–13th 1752 were omitted as Britain had become eleven days out of phase with continental usage.

1753 Hardwick's Marriage Act increased the formalities attendant upon marriage. An act enabling Jews to become naturalized was passed, then repealed because of popular pressure.

1754 Henry Pelham died while preparing for the general election. Hogarth's *The Election* dates from this year.

1755 Johnson's Dictionary was published.

1756 After a reversal of alliances the Seven Years War broke out. In effect Britain and Prussia were fighting France and Austria and Russia. The ministry of Newcastle, Pelham's brother, fell.

1757 A ministry based on a coalition between Newcastle and Pitt replaced the Devonshire-Pitt administration.

1758 Blackstone was elected to the Vinerian Professorship of Law at Oxford and began to deliver his 'Commentaries on the Laws of England'.

1759 In this 'annus mirabilis', British arms were triumphant at Minden, Quebec, Quiberon, Lagos and the capture of Guadeloupe.

1760 George III succeeded his grandfather George II. Sterne's *Tristram Shandy* was published.

Index

Jones, Mr (carpenter, Buckingham), *90*, 140
Jordan, Zachary (ploughwright, Helmdon), *94*

Kent, Mr (attorney, Grantham, Lincolnshire), 100, 101, 102, 107
King, Mr Ben (butcher), 16, *139*

Land, Mr John (Attorney at Law, Buckingham), 18, *19*, *20*, 83, *85*, 86, 118
Launder, Mr, 144
Leapor, Philip (gardener, Brackley), *93*
Linnee, Hannah, 137, 138, 140, 151
Long, Lady (London), *143*
Loveday, Mrs (Brackley), *51*
Low, John (Cold Harbour, Studham),*40*
Lucas, John (Westbury), 14, *73*, *75*

May, William, 81, 82
Meads, Mr (carrier), 16, 20
Meaks, Goodwife, *80*
Meredith, Mr Hugh (Attorney at Law, Lincoln's Inn, London), 122, *123*, *124*, 125, 126, 127, 128
Minshull, Dick (horse racer), 67
Minshull, Mr, 67
Modocks, Mr (secretary to the Duke of Grafton), 162
Montague, Viscount of Sussex, 67
Moor, Sir George (Maids Moreton), 67
Morgan, Mr senior (Lee), 75
Morris, Mr (welldigger, Buckingham), *92*
Moulson, Peter (London), 21, *34*, *50*, *52*, *65*, *114*, *115*, *116*, *117*, 121, 122, 123, 124, 125, *125*, 126, 127, 128, 129, *131*, *132*, *133*, *151*, *158*, *161*, *163*, *164*, *165*
Mulford, Mr (London), 99, *118*, 130, 131
Murray, Colonel, 36

Nicholls, 28
North, Lord, 67

Paddon, Mrs Alice (Holton, Bedfordshire), *143*, 145
Paddon, Thomas, *145*
Paine, Mr James (Jemmy) (Brackley), *8*, *39*, *74*, 138, *166*, *167*
Paine, Oliver (baker, Brackley), *91*
Palmer, Sir Charles, 49
Palmer, Mr (carrier, Brackley), *15*, 30
Parker, Charles (mason, Brackley), 91, *91*, *92*, *93*, *94*
Parker, Mr (barber, Brackley), 39
Pashler, Samuel (Buckingham), *59*
Passelow, Samuel, *62*
Paxton, Mrs, 143
Penell, George, 82
Penell, Goodwife Susannah, 25, 28, 78, 82, 140
Penell, Tom, 78
Perkins, Mr James (Tingewick), *22*, *72*, 77
Pidenton, Mr (Brackley), 139
Pillsworth, Mr, 29, 30
Pitt, Dr, 47
Pollard, John, Esq. (Finmere), *43*, *44*, *45*, *46*, *161*
Porter, Mrs (Miss Cunington), 98, 99, 103
Porter, Ralph (nephew of E.P.), 98, *99*, 99, 100, 101, 102, 103, 104, 105, 106, 107, 108, 113, 120
Porter, Mrs (mother of Ralph P.) (Scarborough), *100*, 103, 108
Postmaster, the, at Cheltenham, 57
Potts, Mr ('the newsman'), 17, 121
Poulton, Catharine (servant), 40
Preston, Mr, 101
Price, Mr Campbell, 14, 44, 116
Price, Mrs Mary (Whitfield), 49, 50, 56
Price, Mrs Susan (Whitfield), *64*
Price, Rev. Mr Thomas (Buckingham), 155
Price, Rev. William (Whitfield), *14*, *65*, 114
Purefoy, George (great grandfather of H.P.), 67

Rawlins, Mr (butcher, Heath), 150
Rayner, Dr (physician, Bath), 57
Read, Mr, 141